ST EDMUND HALL

St Edmund Hall in 1989, with site extending from New College garden to High Street

St Edmund Hall

Almost Seven Hundred Years

J. N. D. KELLY

OXFORD UNIVERSITY PRESS
1989

Oxford University Press, Walton Street, Oxford OX2 6DP
Oxford New York Toronto
Delhi Bombay Calcutta Madras Karachi
Petaling Jaya Singapore Hong Kong Tokyo
Nairobi Dar es Salaam Cape Town
Melbourne Auckland
and associated companies in
Berlin Ibadan

Oxford is a trade mark of Oxford University Press

Published in the United States
by Oxford University Press, New York

British Library Cataloguing in Publication Data
Kelly, J. N. D. (John Norman Davidson, 1909–)
St Edmund Hall: almost seven hundred years.
1. Oxfordshire. Oxford. Universities. Colleges.
St. Edmund Hall History
I. Title   378.425'74
ISBN 0–19–951559–X

Library of Congress Cataloging in Publication Data
Kelly, J. N. D. (John Norman Davidson)
St Edmund Hall: almost seven hundred years / J.N.D. Kelly.
p. cm.
Includes index.
1. St. Edmund Hall (University of Oxford)—History.   I. Title.
II. Title: Saint Edmund Hall.
LF741.S25K45   1989
378.425'74—dc20   89–16042
ISBN 0–19–951559–X

Typeset by Hope Services, Abingdon, Oxon
Printed and bound in
Great Britain by Biddles Ltd,
Guildford and King's Lynn

Preface

THIS small book is in a sense a love-child, the fruit of more than half a century's affectionate relationship between its subject and myself. Like most people linked with St Edmund Hall, I have long been troubled by the lack of an accurate, not too encumbered history—indeed, of any full-dress history at all—of what must count as one of Oxford's oldest and most interesting academical societies. This is a belated attempt to fill the gap. If it has proved more difficult to put together than I originally expected, this is because of the disconcerting dearth of source-material until well into the present century. While many of the colleges have reasonably continuous records, the hall had no formal accounts until 1913/14, no minute-books other than of student clubs until the 1930s. Luckily one or two solid documents like Principal Mill's 'Leiger Book', a few revealing diaries, and some lively collections of letters have been handed down. For whole decades, even generations, however, the historian has to depend on widely separated scraps of evidence which have been fortuitously preserved, as often ás not for purposes unconnected with the hall.

In constructing my story I owe a great debt to A. B. Emden, notably to *An Oxford Hall in Medieval Times*, on which my first three chapters are largely based, but also to the article about the hall and its older buildings which he contributed to the third Oxfordshire volume of the *Victoria County History* and to his many other occasional articles. I have been fortunate in the more personal help which others have given me. Both Jeremy Catto, of Oriel College, and the late Gareth Bennett, of New College, allowed me a pre-publication view of chapters they were preparing for the new *History of the University of Oxford*. Adrian Roberts, Keeper of Oriental books in the Bodleian Library, showed me a lecture he had given on S. C. Malan, and the Revd Peter L'Estrange, SJ, directed me to certain letters of cardinal Newman. Mark Curthoys and Ralph Evans, assistants to the *History of the University* project, have generously supplied me with statistical and other information. John Kaye, archivist of Queen's, gave me a copy of his exhaustive study of the college's benefices, and the librarian of Keble showed me some manuscript letters of Principal Barrow.

Preface

Anthony Marks, warden of Liddon House, let me browse in Liddon's diary. Among fellows of St Edmund Hall both John Dunbabin and Blair Worden read and commented constructively on selected chapters, while Graham Midgley came up with several inspired suggestions for enlivening Chapter XI. Bruce Mitchell recalled for me a revealing prayer of Thomas Hearne. Nicholas Cronk has given advice and practical assistance with the illustrations. John Cowdrey not only read and commented on two or three chapters, but laid open the hall's archives to me; he has also patiently discussed with me a great many points which I have raised with him from time to time. To all these I offer my heartfelt thanks. I should also like to add a warm tribute to Alice Gibbons, who has photocopied all my chapters, some of them more than once, and has spoiled me almost as much as she spoils her goldfish.

J.N.D.K.

Assumption of the BVM, 1988

Contents

LIST OF ILLUSTRATIONS   viii

ABBREVIATIONS   x

   I. Origins and Name   1
  II. Advance, Set-back   11
  III. Recovery, Crisis, Rescue   21
  IV. Elizabethan and Stuart Revival   30
   V. A Golden Epoch   41
  VI. Stand-Still, Revival, Witch-Hunt   56
  VII. Evangelical Interlude   67
VIII. Take-over Threats Averted   87
  IX. War and Post-War Expansion   103
   X. Before and After World War II   110
  XI. From Hall to Mixed College   130

INDEX   151

List of Illustrations

Frontispiece
ST EDMUND HALL. The photograph (J. W. Thomas, May 1989) shows the original quadrangle, with the church–library to the north, the Kelly and Emden buildings to the east, and the Besse building and High Street houses to the south.

1. ST EDMUND OF ABINGDON: FROM A WINDOW IN ST MICHAEL'S CHURCH, OXFORD. Originally in a window over the sedilia on the south side, this panel is now in the east window of the church. While not necessarily a likeness, it is correct in giving Edmund a beard.   8

2. HENRY RUMWORTH, BD, PRINCIPAL. Tonsured, he wears a blue-sleeved mantle, with furred collar and cuffs, over a ruby robe, with a large white purse hanging from his belt. In 1412 he became prebendary of King's Sutton, in Lincoln cathedral, and Horley was a chapelry attached to this prebend. Thanks to Conway Library, Courtauld Institute of Art.   12

3. THOMAS TULLIE, PRINCIPAL. The original portrait in oils belongs to the college, and hangs in the Wolfson Hall. It was presented c.1844 by a direct descendant 'to be hung in the Refectory'.   42

4. THE HALL IN 1675: FROM DAVID LOGGAN'S OXONIA ILLUSTRATA. The photograph, from Bodleian Library Arch. Antiq.A.II.13, was taken by the photographic department of the Bodleian Library, to which thanks are due.   45

5. DR JOHN MILL. The original portrait in oils belongs to The Queen's College, which has kindly allowed it to be reproduced. The college possesses a copy, which hangs in the Wolfson Hall.   50

6. THOMAS HEARNE. The original print belongs to the college and hangs in the Old Library.   54

7. THOMAS SHAW, DD, FRS. The original portrait in oils belongs to the college and hangs in the Wolfson Hall.   60

8. ISAAC CROUCH, VICE-PRINCIPAL. The original portrait in oils belongs to the college and hangs in the Wolfson Hall.   71

9. JOHN HILL, VICE-PRINCIPAL AND EARNEST DIARIST. The original portrait in oils, by John Wood, belongs to the college and hangs in the Wolfson Hall.   75

List of Illustrations

10. H. P. LIDDON, FROM THE CARTOON BY SPY. From a print, coloured and bearing the caption 'High Church', owned by the college. The original was published in *Vanity Fair: A Weekly Show of Political, Social, and Literary Wares* on 16 September 1876. In an accompanying note Liddon is described as a preacher whom 'the men admire to the verge of conviction, the women beyond the verge of adoration'.   84

11. EDWARD MOORE, DD, FBA. The original portrait in oils belongs to the college and hangs in a fellow's room.   88

12. CHARLES FULLMER'S SITTING-ROOM. The original sketch is one of several drawings he included in his diary.   97

13. ARCHBISHOP LANG BLESSES THE CANTERBURY BUILDING. From a photograph in *SEHM* 1934, facing p. 29.   116

14. THE DUKE OF EDINBURGH PRESENTS THE CHARTER. From a photograph in *SEHM* 1957–8, facing p. 42.   113

15. NOS. 46–56 HIGH STREET. The photograph was taken by J. Bowerman, of B. J. Harris, Photographers, in March 1989.   138

Abbreviations

An Oxford Hall	A. B. Emden, *An Oxford Hall in Medieval Times* (Oxford, 1927).
BRUO	A. B. Emden, *A Biographical Register of the University of Oxford to A.D. 1500*, 3 vols. (Oxford 1957–9).
BRUO to 1540	A. B. Emden, *A Biographical Register of the University of Oxford A.D. 1501–1540* (Oxford, 1974).
DNB	*Dictionary of National Biography*
OHS	*Oxford Historical Society*
OM	*Oxford Magazine*
OUG	*Oxford University Gazette*
Pp	*Parliamentary paper*
SEHM	*St Edmund Hall Magazine*
VCH	*Victoria History of the Counties of England, Oxford-shire*, vol. 3 (London, 1954).

I

Origins and Name

I

THE earliest documentary mention of St Edmund Hall by name occurs in a rental of Oseney abbey for the year 1317–18. This large and prosperous Augustinian house, situated outside the city walls some 300–400 yards south-west of St Thomas's church, owned numerous properties in Oxford which it let out profitably as academical halls. The entry[1] in question records that for the *Aula Sancti Edmundi* it was receiving an annual rent of 35 shillings from John de Cornubia, or Cornwall, a master of arts who hailed from Egloshayle in that county.

For much of the medieval period it was academical halls, not colleges, which provided residence for the great majority of scholars, graduates as well as undergraduates, in Oxford. The first three colleges (University, Balliol, Merton) were founded around the middle of the thirteenth century, and by 1450 they had become ten; but to start with they were the preserve of a privileged graduate minority and did nothing to cater for the mass of ordinary students. At the pioneer stage, when scholars first flocked to Oxford in the twelfth century, they had lived scattered throughout the town, normally in small groups but occasionally alone, in rooms hired from citizens; a young man of rank and substance might take over an entire house for himself and his dependants. But from the mid-thirteenth century at any rate residence in private lodgings became increasingly frowned upon. It was conducive, it was frankly acknowledged, to indiscipline and loose living, and fostered brawling and disorder. In the late fourteenth century Chaucer, in his *Miller's Tale*, could still portray his randy 'poure scoler' Nicholas as occupying a bed-sit in John the carpenter's 'hostelrye', but by then he had become an embarrassing anomaly. In 1410, and again in 1421, the university was to ban townsfolk from taking students as tenants, enacting that they must all reside henceforth under proper supervision in halls.

[1] H. E. Salter, *Cartulary of Oseney Abbey* (OHS xci; Oxford, 1931), iii. 139.

Academic halls, or *hospicia*, were recognized lodging-houses or hostels, the recognition coming from the fact that each was governed by a principal who had been duly approved by the university authorities. From the middle of the thirteenth century, if not earlier, it was becoming customary for a master (or bachelor) of arts, with university encouragement, to rent a property for the express purpose of taking in scholars as his tenants; the business was advantageous for him, for it brought both profit and status, and also for the university, since it could rely on him to supervise his tenants' behaviour. The owners of such houses were sometimes private citizens, but much more frequently they were the religious houses in and around Oxford, notably Oseney abbey, the hospital of St John just beyond the east gate, and St Frideswide's priory (now Christ Church) within the walls on the south side. Halls were normally let on a yearly basis, from 9 September to 9 September, and the university exercised a general oversight by requiring all principals to present themselves before the chancellor or his deputy in St Mary's church and provide guarantees for the payment of their rent. Those who did so were granted security of tenure for the subsequent year, and only those halls whose principals complied with this formality were recognized as academical halls.

Rent-rolls and other contemporary evidence indicate that there were at least a hundred halls, probably considerably more, in the first two decades of the fourteenth century. During the next two hundred or so years their number was steadily falling, the result both of a declining student population and of the amalgamation of the halls themselves; in 1469 they were down to sixty-nine. In appearance and layout they hardly differed from the medium-sized or large town house of the period, which in fact was what they were. The typical *hospicium* was a two-storeyed building with a large central room (the refectory) which rose through the two storeys and was open to the roof to let smoke out from the fire, an adjacent service-room and a kitchen, and several small chambers used for study and sleeping. Besides a bedstead little or no furniture was provided; students supplied their own mattresses and bed-linen. Some of the inmates were on full board (*communarii*), others on half board (*semi-communarii*) served at meals and helped out with domestic chores. The population of a hall also included its servants, of whom the indispensable ones were the manciple, who organized supplies and sometimes kept the accounts, and the cook;

in smaller halls these two functions were probably combined. These were normally townsfolk, and did not reside (a fourteenth-century statute forbade them to do so) in their halls.

Each hall formed a distinct community, and several had a regional or even national connection. Just as it had earlier been natural for groups of students from, say, Wales or Ireland, or from Yorkshire, to share lodgings in the town, so the halls which developed from such households often retained a markedly local complexion. But their official recognition by the university meant that the halls were much more than residential hostels: they were academic societies with a regulated, fairly strict pattern of life. A detailed knowledge of this is not available until the late fifteenth century, when a body of aularian statutes approved by the university was compiled; but these are likely to reflect much earlier practice. If the common table was the centre of their life, they also provided, from the fourteenth century at any rate, aularian lectures in the morning supplementary to the public lectures of the schools and, almost certainly, some informal instruction. Recreation was organized on a community basis. There were fixed times for the opening and closing of gates, meetings on Saturday evenings at which, after an anthem and a social break, breaches of the regulations were reported and offenders punished, and strict requirements for attending mass and other services at the parish church. While it is likely that all the members of a hall, especially the graduates, had some voice in the management of its affairs, the responsibility of the principal both for its administration and for maintaining good order was unquestioned.

II

The Oseney rental for 1317–18 reveals that the rents the abbey received for its halls varied enormously, one being as low as 15 shillings, another as high as £4. 6s. 8d; there were several at or about 40 shillings. These figures suggest that St Edmund Hall was then a small to medium-sized establishment. It was also territorially much smaller than (as we shall discover in the next chapter) it was shortly to become, being confined to the western quarter of the existing quadrangle.

We are fortunate in knowing how the abbey came to acquire the site. The entire area of the quadrangle had been purchased *c.*1217

3

by John de Bermingham, a comfortably-off cleric who was then rector of Iffley. He subsequently divided it into four parallel, roughly equal segments running north to south, giving away the three lying to the east to the Benedictine priory of Sandwell, Staffordshire, the Augustinian priory of Wroxton, Oxfordshire, and (the easternmost) the hospital of St John, Oxford respectively. The western segment alongside the lane leading to St Peter's he kept to himself, and in due course it passed to two relatives, Roger de Bermingham, rector of Enfield, Staffordshire, and his brother Sir Brian de Bermingham. In 1261–2 Sir Brian, with Roger's consent, sold it for 12 marks (£8) to Thomas of Malmesbury, perpetual vicar of Cowley. Nine years later (1270–1) Thomas conveyed the site with its buildings to Oseney abbey, retaining a life interest for himself, and then in 1289–90 surrendered this interest and presented the property absolutely to the abbey, subject only to two annuities, one of 13s. 4d. for himself and the other of 8s. for his niece, a nun at Littlemore priory.

Nothing remains of the house John of Cornwall rented on this constricted plot, and we have very few clues to what it looked like, none at all to the number of students it accommodated. It was almost certainly an L-shaped tenement, with its north wing alongside the churchyard stretching to the east wall of the present buttery, its west wing on the lane terminating just before the present entrance (the site of which was then occupied by a shop). Much of it may have been constructed of wattle and daub, and very little of the solid masonry that is now so prominent. It is a fair guess that the north wing had two storeys, with a kitchen and a buttery at least on the ground floor and chambers for the principal and his scholars on the first floor. The west wing may well have already contained the refectory, as it was to do for centuries; but again this is only a guess. The two arms of the L enclosed a narrow strip of yard or garden which the inmates used for growing vegetables. The entrance to the hall from the lane was probably by a covered passage which opened into this yard where the present doorway to the Old Dining Hall stands. The yard was overlooked from the east by the tenement occupying the land given by John de Bermingham to Sandwell priory, which had by now become the property of Wroxton priory, owner of the adjacent strip to the east. On its west side John of Cornwall's hall looked out across the lane on a series of small shops which a few years later, in 1341–5, were to be purchased by Robert de Eglesfield, founder of Queen's, and which would eventually become the great gate and east frontage of his new college.

III

Such later Oseney rentals as survive from the fourteenth century, in the original or in transcript, indicate that the property continued to be let as an academical hall, almost certainly without interruption. While they record its name as St Edmund Hall, several supply an interesting alternative designation, 'Vicar of Cowley's tenement' or the like; these variants recalled Thomas of Malmesbury's benefaction to the abbey. Further, there can be no serious question that it was already an academical hall, two or three years at any rate before 1317–18, for the rental for 1315 or thereabouts (as it is imperfect, its exact date cannot be fixed) describes it as 'the house of Cowley' and notes the payment of the rent (2½ marks = 33s. 4d.) by William Boys. The term 'house' (*domus*) was regularly used to denote a hall, and while Boys is not described as either master of arts or principal, the wording suggests that he was in charge of the hall as acting principal. He was perhaps still a bachelor with two or three years to run before incepting as master. If this point can be accepted, what we should next like to know is when the tenement first became an academical hall.

All the evidence points to a date after it passed into the hands of the abbey, almost certainly in the last decade of the thirteenth century. Earlier dates have been canvassed; they start from the premiss that its previous owners, the Berminghams and Thomas of Malmesbury, very probably used it for housing students. Two of them were local clerics, and it is agreed that in the thirteenth century, when the problem of student accommodation was acute, clergy beneficed in and around Oxford frequently engaged in the lucrative business of letting houses to scholars. We have no means of checking what these particular clerics did with their property, but if one or other, or all, of them used it as a lodging-house, this would be entirely in accord with current practice. But this fact, if fact it was, did not in itself make the house into an academical hall, although it would confirm the tradition of its use for student residence long before the first colleges were founded. When the abbey took over, however, it was to be expected that, as a substantial investor in halls in Oxford, it would convert its new acquisition into one as soon as it was practically possible. It had not done so by 1277, for the rental for that year, which includes St Peter's parish, contains no mention of it; but that is not surprising, since under his deed of 1270–1 Thomas of Malmesbury still retained certain rights over it. We get no help from such rentals as survive between 1277 and 1315, for they are fragmentary, with the section covering St Peter's parish missing. Even so, a date quite soon after 1289–90 seems likeliest, for it was in that year that Thomas conveyed the house absolutely to the abbey. Such a date is perhaps confirmed by the fact that, when the hall at last appears in the rental for 1315, it is designated 'house of Cowley'. This description, which was to cling to it for several decades, strongly suggests that its transference to aularian status took place when Thomas's generous gift was still fresh in people's minds.

IV

One further question remains: how did Oseney's 'house of Cowley' come to be permanently designated St Edmund Hall? The name commemorates the first graduate of the university to become archbishop of Canterbury, the first also to be canonized. A short excursus[2] about him is necessary before the question can be answered.

Born at Abingdon *c.*1170 to comfortably-off parents, Reginald le Rich and Mabel his wife, Edmund as a lad attended a grammar school in Oxford just west of St Mary's church. His schooling finished, he was sent by his strong-willed mother (his father had meanwhile become a monk) to Paris to follow the arts course. After graduating as master, he returned to Oxford and lectured in arts for six years (*c.*1195–1200); Roger Bacon, the philosopher and experimental scientist, reports that he was the first to lecture there on Aristotle's *Elenchi*, thus being one of those who introduced the new logic to the curriculum. Towards the end of this period his deceased, but still dominating, mother appeared to him in a dream, reproved him for demonstrating bizarre geometrical figures in the schools, and on the palm of his hand traced three circles, signifying the persons of the Trinity. This he took to be a sign that he must

---

[2] The following two paragraphs are based on C. H. Lawrence's authoritative *St Edmund of Abingdon: A Study in Hagiography and History* (Oxford, 1960).

dally no longer with secular learning, and so went back to Paris to immerse himself for several years in theology. After a year's residence at the Augustinian priory at Merton, Surrey, he returned to Oxford, incepted as doctor in theology, and lectured on the subect *c.*1214–22. In 1222 he accepted appointment as canon and treasurer of Salisbury, and in 1227 preached the sixth crusade for Pope Gregory IX. It was Gregory who, after rejecting three other candidates, was instrumental in getting him elected archbishop of Canterbury in 1233. It was probably at some date before his consecration (2 April 1234) that he wrote his widely influential mystical treatise *Speculum ecclesie (Mirror of the church)*.

Essentially an ascetic and master of the spiritual life, Edmund had little taste for administration and politics. He nevertheless proved a courageous leader at a time of national crisis, resisting interference by Henry III, mediating between him and the barons, and forcing him by the threat of excommunication to reconstruct his council. The king's reaction was to persuade the pope to name a legate for the kingdom. In autumn 1240 Edmund crossed the channel to France, not (as some early sources suggest) to retreat from the frustrations of public life, but as the first stage of a journey to Rome where he hoped to plead his cause with the pope. Falling ill on the way, he died on 16 November at Soisy (near Provins) and was buried at Pontigny, where his embalmed body is preserved in a gilded baroque casket over the high altar in the great Cistercian abbey. Almost immediately there was a strong popular demand for his canonization, and papal commissions investigated the claims submitted on his behalf. After delays instigated by Henry III and other former adversaries these were eventually accepted, and on 16 December 1245 at the council of Lyons, Pope Innocent IV declared him a saint of the church. The bull of canonization, proclaimed on 11 January 1246, fixed 16 November as his feast-day. His appeal to the mass of ordinary people of those days sprang from their conviction (not usually shared by synodical appointment committees today) 'that those who rule the church should be learned, humble, and holy men'.[3]

So we come back to the question of the hall's name. From the start Edmund's cult was understandably popular in Oxford. One of its chief centres, for example, was St Edmund's Well at Milham

---

[3] C. H. Lawrence, *St Edmund of Abingdon*, 182.

1. St Edmund of Abingdon. From a window in St Michael's Church, Oxford. This panel, executed *c.*1290, illustrates the popularity of St Edmund's cult in Oxford at the time when the hall was starting up. He is correctly represented as bearded

Ford (now in the grounds of St Hilda's College), highly reputed for its healing properties. The crowds resorting to it in the 1280s and early 1300s, and the superstitious practices to which it gave rise, instigated the bishop of Lincoln (in whose diocese Oxford then lay) to impose peremptory bans on it in 1291 and again in 1301. The university was particularly proud of its illustrious son, and no fewer than two academical halls adopted his name, Little St Edmund Hall, situated where Brasenose College chapel now stands, and the hall with which we are concerned. As it happens, the grammar school where Edmund first studied in Oxford, and in which he was said to have once had a miraculous escape from falling masonry, occupied the exact site on which Little St Edmund Hall was to rise a century later. There can be little doubt that it was recollection of these facts that inspired its name. So far as our hall is concerned, it is about as certain as it can be that Edmund lived in the parish of St Peter-in-the-East when he was lecturing in arts at Oxford. The evidence is an important statement by the university in its letter to Pope Gregory IX supporting his canonization,[4] namely that as regent master he had used his lecture fees and other funds at his disposal to erect a chapel in honour of the Blessed Virgin, for whom he had a special veneration, 'in the parish in which he was then residing'. In the time of Anthony Wood, the celebrated Oxford antiquary and historian (1632–95), this was generally held to be none other than the lady chapel at the north-east corner of St Peter-in-the-East, and this identification is borne out both by the architecture, which exactly fits the dates of Edmund's residence, and by the fact that no other parish church in Oxford has a lady chapel which can be plausibly attributed to him.

Linked with this report, though less strongly supported, is an ancient tradition that the hall marks the site of Edmund's actual residence. Embellished versions of this, recorded (though finally rejected) by Anthony Wood, even claim that he 'first instituted St Edmund's Hall', turning his house into 'a place of learning', and that 'he had read to his Scholars therein'. Nothing in his early biographies warrants this elaboration; the suggestion that he had had students regularly boarding with him is indeed refuted by a reminiscence in one of them that once, when a poor scholar of his

---

[4] For the Latin text of this 'letter of postulation' (the original manuscripts are at Sens cathedral) see *An Oxford Hall*, 267–70, and C. H. Lawrence, *St Edmund of Abingdon*, 290–3.

fell ill, he brought him into his house and personally looked after him for some five weeks. The tradition itself, although we have no means of testing it, need not be dismissed out of hand. Whether it is truth or pious fiction, however, it remains a fact that in the early 1240s it was common knowledge in Oxford that Edmund had lived in the parish of St Peter-in-the-East. As we have noted, enthusiasm for his cult was particularly fervent in the last decade of the thirteenth century and the first of the fourteenth. Nothing was more natural than that his name should quickly become attached to the hall which about this time was starting up a few yards from the church near which he had lived and which he had enriched with its splendid lady chapel.

II

Advance, Set-back

I

SUCH information as survives about St Edmund Hall between its first mention in 1317–18 and the middle of the sixteenth century is so fragmentary and discontinuous that no consecutive history of it could be attempted. Fortunately it includes several items, often haphazardly preserved, bearing on its life, its buildings, or individuals belonging to it which enable us to trace its general development in shadowy outline, and its crisis in the reigns of Henry VIII and Edward VI, with slightly more precision. The object of this and the following chapter is to bring together and sort out the more significant of these.

For the remainder of the fourteenth century we must depend on the Oseney rentals, which supply the names of principals at any rate, and on a few other miscellaneous scraps of contemporary evidence. Even the list of principals is disappointingly incomplete because of the disappearance of the great majority of rentals. Thus we know that William Boys and John of Cornwall were succeeded by Robert Luc (or Luke), MA, also of Cornwall, who is mentioned in the rentals of 1319–20 and 1324–5, and that Luc 'gave the principalship' to John de Bere, MA in 1325—a revealing disclosure of the way the office might pass from one holder to another. On the other hand, we have no clue to John de Bere's tenure since all the rentals from 1325 to 1351 have perished. We may note, however, that while William Boys and John of Cornwall are mere names, Robert Luc and John de Bere are known to have been rectors, of parishes in Cornwall and Devonshire respectively, who had obtained leave from their bishops to study at the university. Both succeeded in getting their licences for non-residence renewed several times, Luc (who also practised as a physician) in the teeth of ineffectual protests by his bishop at 'the base, unconscientious way he pursues his medical, or rather mendicant, profession, saving money in one place and making it in another, contrary to his calling'.[1]

---

[1] For Luc see *BRUO* ii. 1176.

2. Henry Rumworth, BD, Principal *c*.1395–*c*.1402. Archdeacon of Canterbury 1416–20. (From the panel of painted glass in Horley Church, Oxon.) Presented by himself on becoming archdeacon, this is the earliest portrait of a principal of the hall

The names of only four other principals survive from the century. According to Anthony Wood, the antiquary, who saw a piece of the 1351–2 rental (now lost), a man called Throp (first name not given) was principal in that year. Then, after an interval of thirty years, the names of William Hamsterley and Edward Upton[2] are recorded, again by Wood, for the years 1381 and 1384–8 respectively. Nothing is known of the former, but Upton wrote several treatises on logic, resided in University College in 1401–2, and from 1402 to *c*.1420 was a Buckinghamshire rector. Finally, after another gap, Henry Rumworth of Cirencester, BD, appeared as principal, according to Wood, on rentals between 1395 and 1399. He probably resigned in 1402–3, when he was elected a fellow of Queen's, where he later became treasurer; he was the first principal to be connected with the college. A man of distinct administrative ability, he was destined for an important career. In 1408 he was appointed king's clerk, and in 1416 archdeacon of Canterbury; as royal chaplain he accompanied Henry V on his French campaigns in 1415 and 1417. A contemporary portrait of him, kneeling and elaborately robed, can be seen in the top light of a window on the north side of Horley church, four miles north-west of Banbury.[3]

Interrupted and meagre though it is, the list of principals can be taken as confirming the continuous use of the tenement as an academical hall throughout the century. An interesting conclusion that emerges is that, during the principalships of John of Cornwall, Robert Luc, and John de Bere at any rate, it was probably the resort of scholars hailing from the west country. There were other houses in Oxford catering for a similar clientele, notably the collegiate hall founded in 1314 by Walter de Stapledon, bishop of Exeter, soon to become Exeter College, but the hiatus in the Oseney rentals prevents us from knowing how long our hall continued to retain this particular regional flavour.

II

Partly from the rentals, partly from other documentary scraps, we are fortunately able to catch one or two precious glimpses of the hall's development in the fourteenth century. First, the rentals show

---

[2] For Upton and his writings see *BRUO* iii. 1932.
[3] For Rumworth see *BRUO* iii. 1607; for the window see P. A. Newton, *The County of Oxford: A Catalogue of Medieval Stained Glass* (London, 1979), 114 and pl. 7.

that whereas the rent paid by John of Cornwall to Oseney in 1317–
18 was 35 shillings, the rent paid by Robert Luc in 1324–5 was
46s. 8d. This sharp increase, at a time when the actual rents paid
for student accommodation were falling, is almost certainly to be
explained by the enlargement of the hall's site in the intervening
period. A substantial enlargement was in fact carried out, and was,
curiously enough, the indirect result of Edward II's shattering
defeat at Bannockburn in June 1314. As the king rode in disarray
towards the coast from the disastrous field, he had vowed to the
Blessed Virgin that he would found a house for the Carmelite friars
if he made good his escape. He fulfilled his vow in February 1318
by presenting Beaumont palace, close by the north gate outside the
city walls, to the Carmelites of Oxford. As they wished to link this
with their original house in what is now Walton Street by taking
over some property belonging to Oseney abbey which lay between,
the king made this possible by arranging with the abbey to give it in
exchange certain lands adjacent to the hall which he had received
from one John de Coleshille, an Oxford citizen of substance. These
were none other than the two plots, roughly covering the central
sector of the present quadrangle, which (as we saw in the last
chapter) John de Bermingham had originally owned and then
presented to Wroxton and Sandwell priories, and which John
de Coleshille's father, Nicholas, had purchased in 1285–6 for
10 marks (£6. 13s. 4d.).

The letters patent granting this messuage to Oseney were issued
on 6 June 1318, and shortly after that the abbey leased its newly
acquired property to the principal of the hall. It is likely that, in
negotiating these complicated territorial exchanges, the abbot and
canons had had precisely this augmentation of their existing
investment in view. For the hall the transaction meant the effective
doubling of the area under its control, the acquisition of increased
residential and other accommodation in the buildings occupying
the site, and the possibility at some later date in the century of
extending its own short building fringing the churchyard. A further
bonus it must have gained was the use of the vitally important well,
now the centre-piece of the quadrangle. The readiness of the
principal to take over the additional terrain and pay the enhanced
rent, which in itself suggests that the hall now ranked with the
larger, if not the largest, halls in the university, can be taken as
evidence of its flourishing state.

Secondly, although the gap is tantalizingly large, the activities of principals some seventy years later suggest that the hall was then enjoying an even more vigorous, thrustful phase. The accounts of Exeter College indicate that both Edward Upton and Henry Rumworth were renting a school from it, the former in 1390–2 and the latter in 1397–8. This was one of the four schools Exeter owned in Schools Street, running north from west of St Mary's; we have no information about the use to which they put it. What is even more significant, in or shortly before 1399 Rumworth greatly extended the premises at his disposal by taking over on lease White Hall, an academical hall which faced on to High Street and occupied the site now covered by a late-twentieth-century collegiate building appropriately named after it. In the late fourteenth and early fifteenth century it belonged to the Bishop family, first to Bartholomew Bishop, a taverner, who had rebuilt the house as a hall in 1381, and then to his son Nicholas. We know of Rumworth's take-over because Nicholas, who kept careful records of all transactions affecting his property, noted that in 1399–1400, with his consent and that of Walter Gode, MA, and of William Wendover, kitchener of Oseney abbey, he had allowed the principal to break through a boundary wall so as to admit of direct communication between St Edmund Hall and White Hall, and that the annual rent due to him from the principal amounted to 35 shillings. These jottings related to the year 30 September 1399 to 29 September 1400, but Bishop left no indication of the date when the lease was first made. As a master was forbidden by university regulations from presiding over more than one hall, it is likely that Rumworth was renting White Hall in the name of Walter Gode, a graduate associated with him. Wendover's consent was necessary as indicating that the abbey acquiesced in this arrangement by one of its town tenants.

The importance of Rumworth's virtual annexation of White Hall can hardly be exaggerated. It had had the rents of its rooms 'taxed', i.e. officially assessed, in 1382, a few months after its adaptation as a hall, and the assessment (preserved by the conscientious Nicholas Bishop) lists six chambers and implies the existence of a refectory, a buttery, and a kitchen. With a frontage of 37 feet on the High, the main range seems to have run about 100 feet from south to north, with two short arms enclosing a narrow courtyard; there seems to have been a garden about 40 feet deep at the north end adjoining our hall.[4] The latrine was probably at the far end of this garden. It was thus a substantial property, somewhat smaller than our hall but probably accommodating ten to fifteen students; the room described in the assessment as 'the principal's chamber' would be occupied by Gode as the graduate deputizing for Rumworth. We have no such detailed catalogue of the rooms available in his main hall, but on the basis of the rental he was paying it has been calculated that it probably housed a slightly larger number. Whether all the rooms were full is another question; but on any reckoning Rumworth's acquisition of White Hall must be considered interesting in view of the fact that in the second half of the century university numbers were well below their earlier peak, and that some halls previously reserved for scholars were either being left empty or were being occupied by laymen.

White Hall continued to be linked to St Edmund Hall for several years. We have no proof that William Taylor, MA, who is named in the rental for 1405–6 and seems to have followed Rumworth as principal, renewed the lease, but Bishop's notes leave us in no doubt that both his successors, Robert Berughdon, MA, and Peter Clerk or Payne, MA, did. According to them, Bishop on 3 October 1408 granted Clerk a lease of the property at a rent of 28s. 4d., stipulating that direct communication between it and St Edmund Hall should be permitted so long as Berughdon 'should occupy the said halls by the title of principal'. Nothing more is known of Berughdon, but Clerk was clearly then a graduate associated with him in whose name he rented the house. Before long, however, Bishop seems to have become uneasy. At some date during William Clynt's chancellorship (October 1408–March 1410) he sought and obtained from him permission to serve formal notice on Clerk terminating the lease. The pretext he advanced was the only one recognized under university regulations when a landlord wanted to restore an academical hall to secular use, namely that he wished to move into the house himself. But although he had obtained his permission, Bishop for some time deferred acting on it. Indeed, his file contains the copy of an agreement, dated 15 May 1411, between himself and Clerk, now described as 'master, principal of St Edmund Hall', relating to the emptying of the cesspool of White Hall. This agreement implies not only that White Hall was still

---

[4] For a convincing reconstruction of White Hall see W. A. Pantin in, *Oxford Studies Presented to D. Callus* (OHS, NS xvi; Oxford, 1964), 58–62.

attached to our hall, but that it might well remain so for at least six more years. Yet before a year and a half had gone by he decided to serve the notice, and Clerk found himself obliged to vacate White Hall by 7 October 1412 at latest.

III

The question at once arises: what prompted Bishop to take steps, hesitantly but in the end decisively, to eject Clerk or Payne (the latter was the name by which he was to be known in the outside world, and which we shall use from now on) from his tenancy? It is conceivable that he genuinely wished, perhaps needed, to reoccupy the premises himself, but it was not many years since his father, at considerable expense, had reconstructed them as a hall, presumably as an investment. It is much more likely that he had quite different considerations in mind, considerations which lift the curtain from one of the most intriguing episodes in the hall's history. In the first decade of the fifteenth century it briefly became a miniature stronghold—one of the last in Oxford—of Lollardy, as the movement spreading the teaching of John Wyclif (c.1330–84), philosopher, theologian, and forerunner of the protestant reformation, was nicknamed.

Wyclif, who had had rooms in Queen's just opposite from 1374 to 1380, had had a keen following among younger dons, and after his death interest in his ideas lingered on in the university sporadically, if on occasion vociferously, in spite of their official condemnation. To archbishop Thomas Arundel it seemed sufficiently dangerous to warrant his summoning a convocation of the southern province in St Frideswide's priory in November 1407, at which the study of Wyclif's writings was heavily censored, and then carrying out, in the teeth of violent protests, a visitation of the university in July 1411. As a result the university found itself forced, before the end of the year, to enact legislation banning Wycliffite teaching and obliging heads of houses to take an oath not to admit anyone suspected of 'heretical pravity or Lollard opinion' to their societies. Against this background it is fascinating to note that two of the principals mentioned in the preceding section, William Taylor and Peter Payne (who is cited as principal in the Oseney rental for 1411–12 as well as in Bishop's memoranda), were notorious and outspoken Lollards. In view of Payne's close association with him it can scarcely be doubted that Berughdon was a Lollard sympathizer too; and as a medieval hall was a small, close-knit community, we may reasonably surmise that the other graduate and undergraduate members of the hall shared their principals' heretical views.

Taylor and Payne were both likely, in different ways, to leave an impress on scholars under their supervision.[5] Born at Aston Somerville, Worcestershire, the former was cited by archbishop Arundel for statements savouring of heresy in a sermon preached at St Paul's Cross in 1406 or 1407, when he was still principal; he was excommunicated for failing to appear. He seems to have quitted Oxford before his excommunication, and to have begun moving about the country in the perilous role of a Lollard preacher. A further citation in 1410 was equally without effect; it described him as a man 'of singular opinions and of the new sect' who set at naught the holy fathers and doctors of the church, and also advocated the seizure of church property. Many years were to elapse, and months of harsh imprisonment, before the inevitable end came. Indeed, on two occasions, in February 1420 and in May 1421, he was induced to recant and was absolved. But on 27 February 1423, having resumed heretical propaganda, he was sentenced by archbishop Chichele to deprivation and degradation as a relapsed heretic. The archbishop himself conducted the ceremony of deposition in St Paul's cathedral on 1 March, and next day, having been surrendered to the secular power, he was burned at the stake at Smithfield, dying 'wyth a mervailous constancy and boldnes' (J. Foxe). He was the first Oxford man to be executed as a heretic.

Peter Payne, born c.1380 near Grantham, was intellectually abler than Taylor, and politically more astute. He had been won over to Wycliffite ideas by an Oxford contemporary, Peter Partriche, whom he later taunted with reverting to orthodoxy when offered a comfortable prebend. Another contemporary, the Carmelite Thomas Netter of Walden, described him as the boldest of the Wycliffites in Oxford. As a young man we find him c.1405 defending the English translation of the Bible sponsored by Wyclif against a Dominican friar. In October 1406 he gained scandalous notoriety by taking the lead in a successful stratagem

---

[5] For them see *BRUO* iii. 1852; 1441–3.

which resulted in letters commending Wyclif's life and teaching, purporting to come from the university and endorsed with its official seal, being sent to his Bohemian admirer and translator, the reformer John Hus (*c.*1372–1415). On 6 November 1410, as part of Arundel's campaign against Lollardy, he was brought before a university committee charged with holding erroneous views on the eucharist, but was acquitted. When and in what circumstances he left the hall is not known, but it was probably in 1412, about the same time as he had to give up White Hall; he must have found the anti-Wycliffite oath imposed in 1411 on heads of houses a stumbling-block. He certainly had a profound influence on Sir John Oldcastle, friend of Henry V and Lollard martyr, but had no part in the rebellion which led to his execution.

What seems abundantly clear is that in autumn 1413, soon after sentence was passed on Oldcastle, Payne himself was cited on a charge of heresy. Rather than face a similar fate, he decided to make his escape from England and seek refuge in Prague. Within three or four years he had become, and for the rest of his life was to remain (in spite of never learning Czech), a leading figure in Bohemian affairs, important both as a theologian and as a diplomat; indeed, his role in securing Bohemia for the Hussites was a key one. In 1433 he attended the council of Basle as one of the Bohemian delegates, making himself conspicuous by his skill in debate and by his wit; the failure of the Bohemians to come to terms with the council should be attributed in large measure to his unyielding attitude. For a time a fugitive, for two years imprisoned and then ransomed, he continued to struggle unremittingly for the unification of the Hussite church, always uncompromising, always moving to ever more extreme positions. He died in Prague in 1455 after forty years of exile.

IV

If Taylor has some claim to be the most courageous of the hall's principals, Payne is the only one to have attained renown in the political life of a distant land. Nevertheless his controversial reputation as a young man at Oxford inflicted a sharp, if temporary, set-back on his hall. Bishop's decision to repossess White Hall, and thereby diminish St Edmund Hall's little empire, was obviously inspired by Payne's involvement with a heresy the authorities were exerting themselves to suppress. It has been suggested that Bishop may have acted at the instigation of Payne's enemies, but there is no proof of this. It is much more likely that he was worried about his own position as the landlord of a tenant so suspect in high quarters.[6]

[6] The manuscript of Nicholas Bishop's jottings belongs to the Cambridge University library. The Bodleian library possesses a transcript, made in 1906 by Herbert Hurst: MS Top. Oxon. d. 72.

III

Recovery, Crisis, Rescue

I

THE hall quickly returned to orthodox paths under Payne's successor, John Darley, BD, who was named as principal (according to Anthony Wood) in the now missing Oseney rental for 1413–14. When bishop Repingdon of Lincoln, himself a former Wycliffite who had long abjured the doctrine, announced in March 1414 his intention to visit the university to root out erroneous teaching, Darley was among the regent masters assembled in congregation to hear his letter read out. Although he remained principal for some eighteen years (1414–32), nothing is known of the hall's history in his time. It is interesting to note, however, that for a decade (1421–31) he combined his office with a fellowship at Queen's, of which he was twice treasurer. On vacating the principalship in 1432, he became rector of Herne, Kent, resigning in 1446 owing to old age. He died in the same year, aged 81, and was buried in his parish church (St Martin's). The fine memorial brass[1] which covers his grave depicts him in the academic costume of a bachelor of divinity; six lines of clumsy Latin verse acclaim his pastoral and scholarly qualities in conventional terms.

From this point, for some thirty-four years, we are able to supplement the Oseney rentals by the earliest surviving register of the chancellor's court;[2] this provides no fewer than seventeen lists recording, with names, the appearance of principals of halls before the chancellor or his commissary to deposit cautions at the annual renewals of their principalships. From these we learn, first, that William Bryton, MA, was principal of our hall (no fewer than fifty-six other halls were represented that year) in 1436, and then that by 1438 John Thamys, MA, had succeeded him. Nothing further is known about Bryton, but we have a fairly full picture of Thamys and his career.[3] It is a reasonable guess that he had been a scholar at

[1] Illustrated in *An Oxford Hall*, facing p. 164.
[2] See H. E. Salter, *Registrum Cancellarii* (*OHS* xciii, xciv; 2 vols., Oxford, 1932).
[3] See *BRUO* iii. 1858–9.

the hall, for his three ordinations in 1434 and 1435 were all on the title of Oseney abbey. After being principal for some twenty years, he became rector of Ross-on-Wye in December 1458 (retaining the principalship for most of 1459), and remained there until his death in 1482. At Oxford he seems to have been recognized as a businesslike person, for he was one of the committee of twelve appointed to raise money for the erection of the Divinity School, and in 1449 he served as keeper of the Turville chest (one of several trust funds from which interest-free loans were made to scholars). He counted as someone of consequence in the town too, being once invited to arbitrate in a dispute between citizens. On several occasions he was chosen as university Lenten preacher, and at least once as preacher for Easter Sunday.

II

Thamys's energetic rule not only reversed the hall's earlier set-back under Payne, but promoted it to one of the largest and most flourishing halls in the university. First, a list of cautions in the register of the chancellor's court reveals that in 1439, soon after taking office, he was, in addition to the hall itself, renting an adjacent garden from St John's hospital. This was the plot now forming the eastern sector of the old quadrangle; it had been given to the hospital, as we noted in Chapter I, by John de Bermingham in the early thirteenth century. The latrine of the hall was located between this garden, for which Thamys was paying a yearly rent of five shillings, and the garden of White Hall. Next, Thamys turned his attention to White Hall itself, and at some date between 1439 and 1444 succeeded in regaining control of it. This we know because the list of principals' cautions for the latter year records that he offered cautions for St Edmund Hall in his own name, for the garden in the name of Nicholas Lethenow, MA, and for White Hall in the name of Thomas Hille, MA. Successive lists of cautions confirm that he continued to rent White Hall for the remainder of his principalship.

Two further ventures which Thamys took in hand brought the hall to its fullest development in the medieval period. At some date between 1446 and 1450 he began leasing St Hugh Hall, with its gardens, from St John's hospital. This was a fair-sized property (its annual rent was 24 shillings) occupying the area now covered by Nos. 42 and 43 High Street; the upper end of its gardens abutted conveniently on the south side of St Edmund Hall. The list of principals' cautions for 1458 records that he held it 'in the name of master Hugh, grammar teacher', which suggests that he used it as a grammar school for fee-paying pupils who would later move on to his main hall. This is confirmed by a later rental of the hospital, which describes it as 'the hall called the Gramerhalle'. Then in 1451 he was enabled to extend the perimeter of St Edmund Hall itself by attaching to it two small properties on Queen's Lane, immediately south of its original buildings, namely a little shop with a room on the first floor which belonged to Oseney abbey and a tiny cottage, recently rebuilt, which belonged to Godstow abbey and of which Oseney had recently taken a lease. These occupied respectively the site of the present gateway and of the most northerly section of the principal's lodgings. The successful completion of this transaction may have been due to the friendly attitude of abbot Thomas Hooknorton, who was noted for his generosity to the university and its halls. In view of this enlargement of its site the abbey raised the annual rent due from the hall from a nominal one of 40 shillings (actually 30 shillings) to 50 shillings.

A determined empire-builder, Thamys expanded the hall to a size it was never again to attain until the middle of the twentieth century. We have no clue to the numbers of the student community over which he presided, but it must have been a reasonably large one, comprising schoolboys as well as undergraduates, to warrant his outlay on rents. He clearly needed, and took steps to provide, an adequate staff of graduates to help him administratively and tutorially; as we have seen, the names of several of these have been preserved in the lists of principals' cautions, and there were doubtless others. In most cases they were probably scholars of the hall who, having taken their degrees, were continuing in residence pending appointment to a suitable benefice. For the repair and upkeep of the fabric of his halls he could look to his landlords, and by a stroke of luck we possess the running accounts of Oseney for almost thirty years from 1452.[4] These give a vivid impression of the wide variety of work carried out, ranging from a new chimney for the kitchen in 1455–6 to the construction of a water-conduit and the clearing of a drain in 1457–8. They also indicate that, since the abbey's expenditure during Thamys's last eight years worked out

---

[4] Bodleian Library, Wood MS F 15.

on average at only 13 per cent of its receipts, it was still getting a highly satisfactory return on its investment.

III

Thamys was a leading figure in the university, and must count as one of the hall's most noteworthy principals. He was succeeded (as we learn from both the Oseney rentals and the lists of principals' cautions) by a former student, Thomas Lee, BD, who had earlier assisted him by supervising, first, St Hugh Hall, then White Hall.[5] Like Thamys, he seems to have been reputed a man of administrative flair, for he was twice appointed curator of university loan-chests and was chosen as junior proctor for the year 1459–60 (the first member of the hall to our knowledge to hold proctorial office). The fact that he continued to lease both White Hall and St Hugh Hall, employing graduates as his collaborators, suggests that he was as successful as his predecessor in managing his academic fief. The names of several of these associated graduates are known to us from the lists of cautions. By chance we can also form some impression of one of his undergraduates, David Turnour, who died in residence in June 1465 and whose affection and trust he had apparently won. In his will David not only made Lee his executor (along with his brother), but bequeathed him 'my better mazer and seven gold nobles of the old coinage, together with my black gown'. He was evidently a young man of substance, with much expensive jewellery, richly ornamented belts, and silver spoons, as well as grammar books and logic books, to dispose of.

Confirmation of the hall's flourishing condition under Lee is provided by the Oseney accounts, which disclose that the abbey expended £10. 2s. 4d and £6. 15s. 9d (sums it would scarcely have thrown away on a faltering enterprise) 'on new building at Edmund Hall' in 1461–2 and 1462–3 respectively. These notes have been the subject of much speculation, but it is a reasonable guess, supported by Anthony Wood's researches in the seventeenth century, that they point to two major building developments. First, the abbey carried out in these years the reconstruction of the cottage and shop on Queen's lane which it had enabled the hall to annex in 1451. Wood mentions the building of 'certain Chambers

---

[5] For Lee see *BRUO* ii. 1123–4.

on the south side' of the refectory; from their position near the entrance passage (which itself was probably created at this time) it has been conjectured that they were intended for the principal's use. Secondly, Wood attributes to this period the erection of a short, two-storey building running east of the refectory along the churchyard, on the site at present occupied by the western half of the north range. This building is clearly visible in Loggan's plan of Oxford (1675); in Wood's day it contained 'a Buttery, Kitchen, and Chambers over them', but when it was pulled down in the 1740s only the fifteenth-century kitchen fireplace was spared. Finally, between 1462 and 1469 the abbey purchased from Magdalen College, which had succeeded to the property of St John's hospital, and permanently incorporated in the site of the hall, the patch of garden at the east end of the present quadrangle which Thamys had begun leasing.

In 1467 Lee was presented to the important rectory of Ewelme, Oxfordshire, and moved there three or four years later; because of gaps in our normal sources the exact date cannot be ascertained. He was succeeded by Richard Broke, BD, who had assisted him as grammar master of St Hugh Hall. It is significant that Oseney abbey, as patron, instituted Broke as vicar of St Mary Magdalen, Oxford, in 1471, and that he combined this busy suburban parish with the principalship till his death in 1500. By itself this suggests a sharp decline in the hall's fortunes, and other pointers confirm this impression. For example, he surrendered White Hall to Magdalen *c.*1489, when the college purchased the freehold from Thomas Barton, Nicholas Bishop's son-in-law; under university rules he could have stuck to it had he wished, or been able, to use it for academical purposes. Again, while he managed to retain St Hugh Hall for several years, the Magdalen rental for 1487 notes ominously that the college had received no rent for it from him 'as it is in a ruinous condition'. There was nothing exceptional in these reverses; the university itself was passing though a severe recession, and the halls, unendowed and fragile, were the first to feel the chill winds. The disastrous run-down of St Hugh Hall must be explained by the brilliant success of the grammar school which William Waynflete, himself a famous schoolmaster, opened in Oxford in connection with his magnificent new foundation of Magdalen College, insisting that it should be entirely free of fees to citizens of the neighbourhood.

IV

With the opening of the sixteenth century the hall entered on a new phase of increasing dependence on Queen's. To any experienced observer total absorption by the college must have seemed its inevitable destiny.

First, with the exception of Humphrey Wystowe, DD, who held office for less than two years (1500–1), and John Pyttes (1508–*c.*1516), who had previously been principal of Magdalen Hall, all the principals between 1500 and 1530 were Queen's men, fellows in three cases, who combined the principalship with their position at the college. They were Thomas Cawse, BD (1501–3), who resigned owing to financial embarrassment; William Patenson, DD (1503–5), who was senior (i.e. northern) proctor for 1505–6; John Cuthbertson, BA (1527–8); and Miles Braithwaite, MA (1528–*c.*1533). The fact that they continued in office at Queen's, while suggestive of an interest on the college's part, does not indicate that it as yet had any proprietary hold over the hall; they were merely following current Oxford practice and supplementing their incomes, no doubt with the college's consent, by assuming additional responsibilities. A point worth noting is that, when Cuthbertson handed his resignation to the pro-vice-chancellor, he requested, in the name of his scholars, that Braithwaite might be his successor. This is the earliest record of scholars of the hall having a voice in the choice of their principal, and illustrates a practice which was becoming accepted in the early years of the century.

Secondly, however, in 1531 or very shortly before, Queen's itself stepped in and secured a lease of the hall from Oseney abbey at a rent of 13s. 4d. a year. Under this new arrangement, while the college of course received room-rents from the residents, it was responsible for repairs to the fabric. The hall was evidently in a dilapidated condition, for the cost of tilers (for the roof), plasterers, and carpenters amounted to about £3 in the first year against only £1. 10s. 10d. received in rents. The abbey must have been relieved to find a corporate body willing to take on the tenancy; halls were no longer a profitable form of investment, and the rents of the few that remained had slumped drastically owing to the dwindling demand for their accommodation. The motives of Queen's in embarking on what was at best a marginally remunerative venture are easy to conjecture. Fee-paying undergraduates were a class for which the older colleges had not hitherto reckoned to cater, but which was now increasingly looking to them rather than to halls for the benefits of residence. Like some of its sisters, Queen's must have found the acquisition of a dependent hall supervised by one of its fellows an admirable solution to the problem of accommodating this novel clientele.

The hall's precarious plight in this period is underlined by the way the principalship was more than once left vacant for several years both before and after 1531. Thus when Braithwaite resigned in September *c*.1533, he was succeeded by William Robertson, BD, a senior fellow of Queen's, but he vacated both offices in November on being instituted vicar of Aldermaston. Thereafter the principalship remained unfilled until January 1538, when Ottwell Toppynge, BD, fellow of Queen's and treasurer 1533–5, twice curator of university loan-chests, offered himself for it, frankly informing the vice-chancellor that the hall had for years been without a head 'to the loss and reproach of our academy'. The running accounts of Queen's add to the gloomy picture, noting that it had received from the hall in room-rents no more than 13*s*., 5*s*. 4*d*., and 12*s*. 6*d*. in 1536–7, 1537–8, and 1538–9 respectively; the number of actual residents for the last year seems to have been down to three. These pitiful figures reflect a paralysis which at this time was creeping over the university as a whole. Little wonder that Toppynge soon decided to give up his gallant attempt to arrest the hall's decline, and retired to a Wiltshire rectory. A successor was found in Thomas Peyrson, MA, treasurer of Queen's, who at his admission on 21 September 1540 declared (the formula he employed marks a constitutional innovation) that he had been elected by the provost and fellows of the college, 'with whom the appointment lies'. Peyrson was to continue as principal and fellow for a few more years, but in the meantime national events were combining with local squabbles to throw the hall's entire future into the melting-pot.

V

On 17 November 1539 the abbey of Oseney, a victim (one of the last) of Henry VIII's Act for the Dissolution of the Greater Monasteries, was surrendered with all its property, including of course our hall, into the hands of the king's commissioners.

Queen's at once took appropriate legal steps to secure its lease, but in fact this proved to be in no danger, for the moment at any rate. Henry's original plan was to convert the magnificent abbey church of Oseney into the cathedral of a new diocese of Oxford, making the last abbot its first bishop. For some five years, therefore, the college continued to pay the annual rent for the hall to the recently constituted chapter. But Queen's now found itself, following the election of William Denysson as provost in January 1541, rent by a furious internal quarrel involving three fellows—Peyrson, Robert Tryffing, and Ralph Rudde—who objected strongly to him. Denysson reciprocated their hostility, assembled damaging dossiers against them, and by 1545 had secured their expulsion or departure. Peyrson, who had tried to safeguard his position as principal by getting himself readmitted formally in August 1542 (this time as nominee of the scholars of the hall, not of the college), retired to a Hampshire rectory, but Rudde,[6] a fellow since 1534 who had been successively camerarius and treasurer, was in no mood to knuckle down. Crossing the lane, he contrived to get himself admitted in 1545 or thereabouts as principal of the hall, and resolved to use it as a base for wreaking his vengeance on Denysson.

By now further changes were afoot. In May 1545, the king having decided to translate the new see of Oxford to St Frideswide's (now Christ Church), the dean and chapter of the short-lived cathedral of Oseney were dissolved and practically all their endowments transferred to the new foundation. The sole exception, apparently, was our hall, which was disposed of independently, being sold on 22 November 1546 to John Bellow, of Great Grimsby, in Lincolnshire, and Robert Bygott, of Wharram, in Yorkshire, both satellites of Thomas Cromwell, vicar-general and chief instrument of the king's ecclesiastical policy, and both notorious speculators in monastic property. Then on 12 December of the same year the site and buildings were resold to William Burnell, gentleman, of London. It remains a tantalizing question why, almost certainly alone of the abbey's properties, the hall was not handed over to Christ Church, but was put up for sale separately. The most plausible conjecture is that the person responsible was none other than Ralph Rudde who, out of bitter animosity to the college and his *bête noire* Denysson, contrived for

---

[6] For the few facts known about him see *BRUO to 1540*, 494.

the hall to be placed beyond the reach of Queen's, which would normally have retained its lease had it passed to Christ Church.

If this conjecture is correct, the provost was quick to counter his machinations, for on 2 February 1553 he purchased the freehold from Burnell for £20. Although the feud between him and Rudde continued with redoubled ferocity, he could do nothing to eject his tormentor so long as he complied with university regulations and punctually paid his rent; but he was prepared to bide his time. Rudde almost certainly remained principal (he was also rector of Copredy, Oxfordshire, and from 1550 of St Ebbe's, Oxford) until his death in June 1557. Within a few weeks of this, on 28 July, Denysson executed a conveyance transferring the site and buildings of the hall from himself in his personal capacity to the provost and fellows of Queen's corporately; on the following day the college, with all its officers present, took formal possession of the property.

The transaction evidently gave great satisfaction to the authorities, for on 1 March 1559, following a direction of convocation, the university in congregation made a composition[7] with Queen's under which it recognized the right of the provost and fellows to elect the principal from time to time, subject to their choice being approved by the chancellor or his deputy, and subject also to their being empowered to visit the hall, like other halls, and to eject the principal if they deemed him unsatisfactory in any way. That this arrangement involved an exceptional privilege was made plain ten years later (1570), when the right to appoint the principals of the six other halls which had survived into the reign of Elizabeth I was firmly vested in the chancellor of the university, notwithstanding the fact that they too all belonged to colleges. The terms of the composition make it clear that the university's reason for according Queen's this privileged standing was its recognition that the college, first, had at great expense prevented the hall from being converted to unworthy purposes and, secondly, had undertaken to preserve it 'henceforth for ever for literary uses'. Thus by his far-sighted intervention Denysson, who died within four weeks of the granting of the composition, had proved a generous benefactor not only of his college but also of the hall, whose security and continuity he had ensured at a time when they were in gravest jeopardy.

[7] For the Latin text see *An Oxford Hall*, 299–300. The original is in the archives of Queen's.

IV

Elizabethan and Stuart Revival

I

DURING his embattled principalship Ralph Rudde had let the hall sink to a depressingly run-down condition. When vice-chancellor Oglethorpe conducted a census of the university in 1552, the return made for 'Edmonde Hall' comprised the principal, one resident graduate, six students, and a manciple—nine names only, in contrast to totals varying from twenty-three to forty-nine returned by the six other halls. In spite of the stability introduced by the composition of 1559 it was slow in making a recovery. The fault for this lay with Queen's, which made no appointment to the principalship for several years. Perhaps it was debating what use to make of its new dependency. There is certainly no evidence that it was lacking in interest; on the contrary, the college long rolls for 1558–60 and 1562–4 (also for 1567–8) demonstrate that it went to considerable expense on the repair of the buildings.

When in 1564 the college eventually elected a principal, its choice was a surprising one. The man nominated was Thomas Lancaster, BD, an extreme protestant, author of a polemical tract on the eucharist, who had been consecrated bishop of Kildare in 1549, had been deprived (owing to his being married) under catholic Mary I in 1554, but since 1559 had been treasurer of Salisbury cathedral and chaplain to Elizabeth I. Sir William Cecil, the queen's secretary of state, was friendly with him, and once described him as 'a lusty good priest'. Admitted as principal on 26 February 1565, he crossed to Ireland in the same year with the new lord deputy, Sir Henry Sidney, and became immersed in Irish affairs, continuing however to hold various benefices in England and Ireland in plurality (he had a royal licence to absent himself from his spiritual offices). Apart from his installation, he never resided at the hall, and resigned the principalship in 1568 on being promoted archbishop of Armagh. He nevertheless retained a soft spot for it, and as he lay dying at Drogheda in December 1583, 'crazed and sycklye after his travell thyther' and surfeited 'with red herring and drinking of mutch sack', he made a will providing for the establishment of a free grammar school in the town to which eight exhibitions tenable at the hall were to be attached. The will, alas, was contested, and so his good intentions came to nothing. The fact that he had powerful friends at Elizabeth's court in a position to apply pressure to Queen's may supply the key to his inexplicable appointment.[1]

After Lancaster's resignation Queen's adopted the policy it was to follow for more than 350 years, almost invariably appointing to the principalship fellows or ex-fellows or others connected with the college. For them it was a highly coveted position. The income they could look for, derived largely from room-rents and other charges (they were landlords as well as dons), was modest but superior to that of the average fellowship; around 1690 it was reckoned,[2] on the basis of there being twenty commoners in residence, at £30 a year, midway between £60 at Magdalen Hall and £10 at Gloucester Hall. But they normally supplemented it by holding one or more livings. Their consequent periodical absences resulted in the vice-principalship being a necessary, responsible office, and until quite recent times vice-principals were sometimes liable to play a key role in guiding the hall's fortunes. The principalship had two further attractions to fellows of Queen's. First, principals of halls were persons of consequence in Oxford, counting as heads of houses and, from 1631, as members of the hebdomadal board, which in effect ran the university. Secondly, under the new protestant dispensation it was open to them, unlike college fellows, to marry. The unique right of Queen's to elect the principal of our hall was indeed challenged in 1601 by a Mr Justice Walmsley, who apparently wished to secure the succession for his son Henry, a fellow of Brasenose, but a commission of inquiry set up by the chancellor unanimously ruled that the composition of 1559 had definitively established it, and that both prior to and since the composition the college had been regularly responsible for appointments.

While two or three of the principals elected in the span from Elizabeth to the Commonwealth were men of little importance, the majority were above average in quality, some of them attaining positions of significance in contemporary society. Philip Johnson,

---

[1] He has a full notice in *DNB*.
[2] See Bodleian Library, Tanner MS 338, fos. 203ʳ–204ᵛ. See also *VCH*, 330 n. 21.

MA (1572–6), for example, left to become domestic chaplain to Edmund Grindal, Elizabeth I's ill-fated archbishop of Canterbury. John Aglionby, DD (1601–10), was chaplain-in-ordinary to both Elizabeth I and James I, and had the reputation of being 'a most polite and learned preacher'; he was reported by Anthony Wood,[3] the antiquary, to have had 'a most considerable hand in the translation of the New Testament' for the Authorized Version of the Bible. Dr John Rawlinson (1610–31), rector of Taplow, a former fellow of St John's, was elected as a result of pressure from the chancellor, archbishop Bancroft, himself a St John's man; he too was 'a fluent and florid preacher', and was appointed prebendary of Salisbury and chaplain-in-ordinary to James I. Much the ablest administrator, however, among these early appointees of Queen's was Henry Robinson, MA (1576–81). Elected at the early age of 24, he retained his fellowship at Queen's, and as senior fellow took the lead in easing out the corrupt provost, Bartholomew Bowsfield, in 1581.[4] He then resigned from the hall and became provost himself, not only restoring order to the college's crippled finances but in 1584 negotiating its re-foundation. Chaplain to archbishop Grindal, with the ear of the statesman Sir Francis Walsingham, he proved an energetic and capable bishop of Carlisle from 1598 until his death from plague in 1616, taking part in the Hampton Court conference in 1604.

II

It was probably Robinson who, in his brief reign, brought the hall to life again after a decade of stagnation; his task was made the easier by the impressive, if irregular, growth in numbers of admissions to the university from 1550 onwards, and by the increasing eagerness of the nobility and gentry to send their sons to it. Although the three principals (Nicholas Cooke, MA, Nicholas Pullen, MA, and Philip Johnson) appointed by Queen's as immediate successors to Lancaster were birds of passage, the hall was already beginning to forge links with the north of England, the fruits of the college's north-country connection. A striking illustration was Robinson's acceptance in his first year of George Carleton, son of a Cumberland squire, favourite pupil and later

---

[3] *Athenae Oxonienses*, ed. P. Bliss (London, 1815), ii. 61.
[4] See J. M. Kaye's article in *The Queen's College Records*, vi (Oxford, 1985), 1, 12–16; also *DNB*.

biographer of Bernard Gilpin, the so-called apostle of the north. Admired at Oxford as a poet and a disputant, Carleton as bishop of Llandaff was to make his mark at the synod of Dort (1618–19) and soon after to be promoted to the see of Chichester; he was the first hall graduate, so far as is known, to attain episcopal rank. As a result of Robinson's efforts the hall began to acquire a creditable reputation, and when the vice-chancellor in May 1579 called for returns of their numbers from all the halls, his vice-principal was able to report that there were no fewer than thirty commoners on the butler's books.

Robinson was succeeded by Thomas Bowsfield, MA (1581–1601), nephew (probably) of the displaced provost of that name, who had made his young kinsman's appointment to the principalship a condition of his own resignation. Thomas was a graduate of Pembroke Hall, Cambridge, whom his uncle had installed as logic lecturer at the college in 1577. Under him the hall's revival seems to have accelerated, for he felt able to launch out on a bold programme of expansion. First, there is some evidence[5] that, at a date which cannot now be ascertained, he put up the small tenement, sometimes called the cottage, which still stands at the south-east corner of the old quadrangle, linked since the 1680s with the chapel. Secondly, 'about the year 1596', according to Anthony Wood[6] (supported by Hearne), he erected the four-storey eastern half of the range of buildings now flanking the north side of the quadrangle (the western half still consisted of a two-storey fifteenth-century building) on ground which had previously formed part of the garden. These additions must have vastly increased the accommodation at his disposal; it is little wonder that Hearne complimented him on having done 'much good' at the hall, while Miles Windesor, a contemporary fellow of Corpus, remarked[7] that 'he renewed his hall from its very foundations'.

Bowsfield's object in carrying out these works must have been to cater for the growing inflow of fee-paying commoners of the better-off class whom he hoped to attract, thereby augmenting his own and his successors' emoluments. We know the name and career of at any rate one such whom he admitted in 1592: David Jenkins, of

[5] See A. B. Emden's article in *VCH*, 320a.
[6] *The History and Antiquities of the Colleges and Halls in the University of Oxford*, ed. J. Gutch (1786), 668.
[7] See T. Hearne, *Collections*, xi. 19.

Glamorganshire, who was destined to become a learned Welsh judge and fanatical royalist, a patron too of Welsh bards who presided at his local eisteddfod. Unfortunately, in his eagerness to raise funds to finance his constructions, Bowsfield seems to have resorted to a variety of shady practices, such as guaranteeing the manciple and other servants security in their jobs in return for substantial monetary gifts, letting out rooms (contrary to university regulations) to townsfolk, and even temporarily transferring the principal's income and functions for ready cash to a former commoner. Towards the end of 1600 the vice-chancellor instituted an inquiry into these allegations, to which were added charges of gross absenteeism, 'especially in the terme tymes', as a result of which 'there hath bine great neglecte of the ordinarie lectures, disputations, and other exercises required by the Statutes of the saide Hall, and of the devoute frequentinge of devine prayer'. It is significant that he held two benefices in far-away Kent, and in 1582 had become a prebendary of Salisbury. Although he put up a defence, the case against him was a damning one, and he decided to cut his losses; on 26 February 1601 he resigned from the principalship.[8]

We have already noted that Bowsfield's successor, John Aglionby, DD, who was elected without delay after the rejection of Mr Justice Walmsley's challenge to the right of Queen's to make the appointment, was an accomplished New Testament scholar. In 1605 he was selected to take part in the divinity disputations which the university put on to entertain James I during his official visit. While principal he held two livings in Oxfordshire (Bletchingdon and Islip), and in 1607 obtained permission from the crown (he knew his way around the court) to hold a third, subject to his supplying a suitable curate when unable himself to reside. Under him the hall must have continued to flourish, for in 1605 it was reported[9] to have thirty-eight members on its books. Soon after this date, however, he had to face trouble over the cottage which his predecessor had had built at the south-east corner of the quadrangle, for the innkeeper of the Angel in High Street, who also rented from Magdalen College the King's Arms (which occupied the site of what is now Staircase 8), successfully contended that

---

[8] See the full dossier of the affair in OU Archives, *Visitationes Aularum*, D. 26. 3, fos. 54ʳ–73ʳ.
[9] Cf. A. Clark, *The Life and Times of Anthony Wood*, iv. 150–1.

Bowsfield had encroached on the timber-yard behind the latter tavern. As as result Aglionby was obliged, in December 1608, to take a forty-year lease of the 'lately erected' tenement from Magdalen at a rent of five shillings a year. The college rent-rolls indicate that he made it his residence when in Oxford. Although it was to pass into private hands in 1636, the property was destined, through the intervention of Queen's, to belong permanently to the hall, for in 1673 the college took the first of a series of forty-year leases of it and eventually, in 1783, purchased the site from Magdalen for the benefit of its dependent neighbour.

III

On the day following Aglionby's death (6 February 1610) at the early age of 43, Queen's elected, as usual, one of its fellows, Barnabas Potter, to succeed him, but he, for reasons unexplained, resigned before being admitted to office; he went on to become provost, and later bishop of Carlisle. Unfortunately for the college, he tendered his resignation 'into the hands' of the chancellor, archbishop Bancroft, who seized his chance (as we have seen) to press on it a protégé of his own without any Queen's connection. When the college remonstrated, 'he promised them very fair for the next avoidance', but this time got his way.[10] Although Dr John Rawlinson resigned his Taplow rectory, he was soon presented to the rectories of Selsey, Sussex, and Whitchurch, Hampshire. He must have been a busy man, for while he is reputed to have spent a lot of time in Oxford, 'he was much followed' in those parishes 'by his frequent and edifying preaching, and great charity and public spirit'.[11] Not long after his installation at the hall, on 19 April 1613, it had to receive a visitation by the vice-chancellor, one of a series to which the halls were subjected in the reigns of Elizabeth I and the first two Stuarts. They illustrate the stricter standards of teaching, administration, and discipline to which they, with the whole university, were now being required to conform. On this occasion, besides the principal, there were present six MAs (three of them beneficed, 'all preachers'), three BAs, eight of the twenty undergraduates who had their names on the books, the manciple, the butler, and the cook.

---

[10] Cf. W. Scott and W. Bliss (edd.), *The Works of William Laud* (Oxford, 1847–60), v. 34–5.   [11] A. Wood, *Athenae Oxonienses*, ii. 505–6.

Both the vice-chancellor's searching questionnaire, clearly based on the aularian statues of the day, and the responses of the principal's six representatives survive in full,[12] and provide a fascinating picture of life and conditions in the hall in the early seventeenth century. All aspects of the community were covered by the inquiry, from religious observance to academic exercises, from the behaviour of students in hall and in the town to the payments for which they were liable and the meals they consumed. All the undergraduates, it was claimed, had tutors, and proper provision was made for 'lectures, disputations, theames, and such like', and for 'weekelie corrections' (i.e. sessions for discipline); but it had to be admitted that bachelors and scholars were negligent in speaking Latin among themselves, while junior members generally failed to pay due respect to doctors and other higher graduates. Morning prayer was said daily between 5 and 6 a.m., on Sundays and holy days at 8; grace was said before and after meals, and a bible clerk read a chapter at dinner. Every precaution was taken to ensure that there were no lurking vestiges of 'Papistrie', e.g. that no 'popishe prohibited books' were allowed, no 'holidaies or fasting daies abrogated by authority are . . . superstitiouslie observed', and that no attempt was being made to 'seduce anie youth . . . to goe to the seminaries beyonde the seas'. There were separate tables for masters and bachelors, although commoners could sit at them if they presented a piece of plate 'for the use of the house' and paid a regular fee. The possession of guns, daggers, and crossbows, and the frequenting of taverns, tobacco shops, and disorderly places, were frowned upon, as were the keeping of dogs, hawks, or ferrets and the wearing of 'longe or shagged haire' and 'unseemlie apparrell'. The gate was ordinarily shut just after 9 p.m., and undergraduates were not expected to walk into town without permission. No junior member was allowed to reside or take meals outside the hall, and it was insisted that the 'allowance of breadde, drinke, and meate be holsomlie and reasonablie provided'. It was estimated that, with the exception of sons of noblemen or knights, scholars spent five shillings a week on battels, being punished by the principal if they exceeded this.

We have no idea what proportion of Rawlinson's charges were sons of noblemen or knights, but three at any rate were to make

[12] See OU Archives, *Visitationes Aularum*; also, for a complete transcription by A. B. Emden, *SEHM* (1929), 59–66.

their mark in later life. Two of these, George Bate (1608–69) and William Berkeley (1606–77), were migrants from Queen's who perhaps found the hall more economical. Bate took his BA through the hall in 1626, going on to graduate both BMed and DMed, and to become a renowned doctor. He was personal physician to Charles I during his stay in Oxford, and under the Commonwealth to Oliver Cromwell, whom he attended on his deathbed; at the restoration he turned royalist again and was appointed physician to Charles II. One of the earliest fellows of the Royal Society, he lectured on anatomy at the Royal College of Physicians. Berkeley,[13] brother of John, first baron Berkeley of Stratton, a polished courtier and amateur dramatist, took his BA through Queen's in 1624, and after a time at the hall moved to Merton as a fellow. Knighted by Charles I in 1639, he spent most of his life from 1642 as colonial governor of Virginia, being briefly deposed when the Commonwealth fleet arrived (he had been making the colony an asylum for cavaliers and persecuted clergy). 'Animated by a spirit of almost preposterous loyalty to the throne', he latterly wielded his powers in Virginia so harshly that Charles II exclaimed, 'The old fool has killed more people in that naked country than I have done for the murder of my father.'

The third, Matthew Nicholas (1594–1661), migrated to the hall from New College after taking his BCL degree there in 1620; his chamber-mate was his cousin, John Ryves, also a New College graduate. He resided at the hall until 1627, having taken his rooms on a seven-year lease,[14] 'for which I give £4 fine and £4 yearly rent'; this he complained was 'too harde a bargaine'. He was younger brother of Sir Edward Nicholas, secretary of state to Charles I and then to Charles II, and himself a Queen's man. Our Nicholas was named dean of Bristol in 1639 and canon of Westminster in 1642, but was deprived at the rebellion. His fortunes revived at the restoration, and in 1660 he was promoted dean of St Paul's, but he only lived to hold the office for a year.

IV

Rawlinson died at his Whitchurch rectory on 3 February 1631. He had remembered the hall in his will, leaving it (a benefaction the

---

[13] See *Dictionary of American Biography*.
[14] For these particulars see *VCH*, 328a.

college still enjoys, although inflation has sadly eroded its value) a quitrent of £6 a year on land he owned at Cassington, near Oxford, 'for the mayntenance of a Divinitie Lecture'.

Queen's acted swiftly on hearing of his death, and on the day following elected Adam Airay, BD, a former fellow who was then vicar of Sparsholt, a college living in Berkshire. The election was conducted with unusual precautions, including the presence of a notary public. Ever since Rawlinson had been forced on it, the college had been concerned about its unique privilege. It had spent money on procuring an authenticated copy of the composition of 1559 from the university registrar, and must have been the moving force behind a letter which the chancellor, the earl of Pembroke, addressed in 1626 to the vice-chancellor confirming its right to appoint the principal.[15] Even so, the haste of the election irritated the new chancellor, William Laud (then bishop of London), who complained that it might have been carried out 'with more respect for me and less hazard to themselves'. On being further briefed, however, he confessed that the college's right was 'unquestionable', and authorized Airay's installation.[16] This ought to have settled the matter, but when Laud's revised statutes for the university were promulgated in 1636 the aularian section (by which the halls were to be governed until 1835) contained no mention of any special privilege belonging to Queen's, simply prescribing that principals of halls should be elected by their members (always a dead letter) on the chancellor's nomination. Queen's had protested in vain against the omission, and the provost signed the college's official copy of the code with the proviso 'saving the rights of this college in relation to St Edmund Hall'.

Like Bowsfield before him, Airay was ambitious to expand his hall, at any rate for a few years. First, he took in hand the reconstruction of the oldest portion of what are now the principal's lodgings, pulling down and completely rebuilding (according to Anthony Wood)[17] the 'very ruinous' rooms 'on the south side of, and over, the common entrance into the Hall'. 'Those Edifices now standing in their place' were put up 'at his own charges . . . and finished about 1635'. Secondly, on 1 September 1636 he took a

[15] See J. R. Magrath, *The Queen's College* (Oxford, 1921), 230–1; 253.
[16] See *The Works of William Laud*, v. 35–6; vi. 294–6.
[17] *The History and Antiquities of the Colleges and Halls in the University of Oxford*, 667.

forty-year lease from Magdalen College of the site (at present occupied in the main by Nos. 42 and 43 High Street) on which the grammar hall which principals Thamys, Lee, and Broke had rented in the fifteenth century had stood. It is intriguing to note that the rent he was required to pay was exactly the same, 20 shillings a year, as had been demanded 150 years previously.[18] It has been suggested[19] that Airay may have used these latter premises as his own residence, but we cannot confirm this. What seems clear is that his object in making these enlargements and acquisitions must have been to provide accommodation for an increasing inflow of students he hoped to attract to his hall. Any such plans he may have had, however, were doomed to frustration by the political crisis of the 1640s and 1650s, and its dire impact on the university.

From 1642 to 1646 Oxford was the royalist headquarters in the civil war, in June 1646 it was surrendered to the parliamentary forces, and from June 1647 until April 1658 the university was subject to an exhaustive, though progressively relaxed, visitation by parliament. Inevitably admissions to colleges fell steeply in the 1640s, as did the numbers graduating. The halls, lacking the stability of colleges, were particularly hard hid; the majority ceased to function for a time as academic societies, and hired out their rooms to 'laics'. At St Edmund Hall matriculations, which had been five in 1641, fell to one, one, and two in 1642, 1643, and 1644 respectively. There was none at all in any of the years from 1645 to 1659, although admissions were strongly reviving at the colleges generally by 1650–1, as well as at Magdalen Hall and New Inn Hall, whose relatively flourishing state reflected their puritan complexion. Wood states[20] that after the surrender of the royalist garrison 'there were very few or no students in that hall, only some of Queen's College that lodged there'; and his further report that the refectory at this time 'looked old and ruinous' confirms its run-down condition.

In some degree Airay must be held responsible for the hall's failure to share in the general upsurge of university life in the 1650s, which was very evident next door at Queen's. His name was conspicuously absent from the meagre list of three residents

[18] See *Cartulary of the Hospital of St John the Baptist* (OHS lxvii, 1915), i. 312.
[19] See *SEHM* (1925), 19.
[20] *Athenae Oxonienses*, iii. 1056; A. Wood, *The History and Antiquities of the Colleges and Halls in the University of Oxford*, 667.

(two of them made their submission) who appeared before the parliamentary visitors. He took no active steps to resuscitate the hall, but remained, apparently undisturbed, at his vicarage at Sparsholt until 1653, when Queen's appointed him rector of Charlton-on-Otmoor, Oxfordshire, another college living. He died there on 15 December 1658, and was buried in the church; there survives[21] a detailed account of the expenses incurred in connection with his funeral by his nephew Christopher Airay.

[21] See *SEHM* (1926), 24–6.

V

A Golden Epoch

I

THOMAS TULLIE, BD, elected and admitted as principal on 22 December 1658, only a few days after Adam Airay's death, proved the right man to reverse the decline the hall had experienced for almost two decades. A fellow of Queen's, when the provost had described him ten years before as 'a very hopefull young man', he had retired to a schoolmastering job at Tetley, Gloucestershire, during the royalist occupation of Oxford, but had returned to the college after the surrender of the city to parliament, had readily made his submission to the visitors, and had taken an energetic part in building up the college's depleted numbers. Immediately prior to his appointment, he seems to have been briefly incumbent of a living (name unknown) which he did not find 'very gratefull to him' as there were 'some turbulent Anabaptists' in the parish.[1] A good scholar, author of several treatises and controversial pamphlets,[2] he was appointed chaplain-in-ordinary to Charles II in 1660 as well as being created DD, but thereafter was held back (much to the hall's advantage) by his strict calvinist sympathies from the promotion he deserved, and hoped for, until the year before his death. As well as being principal, he was also rector of Grittleton, Wiltshire, from 1658.

Once installed, Tullie with characteristic vigour demolished the refectory, then in a dilapidated state,[3] and replaced it with a new one (now called the Old Dining Hall), with a warren of rooms above it. Completed in 1659, this building was one of the very few erected in Oxford during the Commonwealth. A list of benefactors who contributed to its construction survives in the Bodleian;[4] it includes George Bate,[5] the aularian physician who had recently

---

[1] See *SEHM* (1943–8), 39–40.
[2] His principal works are listed in *DNB* (s.v. Tully).
[3] Cf. A. Wood, *The History and Antiquities of the University of Oxford*, 667.
[4] Bodleian Library, Wood MS F 28 fo. 306^{r-v}.
[5] See above p. 37.

3. Thomas Tullie, Principal 1658–75

attended the dying lord protector, and Tullie himself, who gave the huge sum of £200. The refectory itself was slightly shorter than its appearance today would suggest, for the panelled screen at the north end stood some five feet to the left of the entrance, which opened on to a narrow lobby, while the space above now occupied by a gallery consisted of two rooms.

At the same time Tullie's energetic policies resulted in a rapid and sustained increase in the number of undergraduates at the hall. By 1662 annual admissions amounted to twenty, and by 1667–8 to twenty-nine; the poll tax returns show that in the latter year the hall had some sixty-five names on its books (a larger total than the returns given for University College, Balliol, Oriel, Corpus, or Pembroke, or for St Mary Hall, New Inn Hall, or Hart Hall). If short of accommodation, as they were sometimes bound to be, he and his successors were able, between 1666 and 1694, to rent rooms in a five-storeyed tenement which Christopher Airay, nephew of his predecessor Adam Airay, had built as a speculation in the former year on the northernmost portion of the messuage his uncle had leased from Magdalen College[6] (the site at present occupied by the building constructed as a library in 1926). It is little wonder that Andrew Allam, who had been an undergraduate at the hall under Tullie and was to assist his successor as vice-principal, reported[7] that during his principalship the hall 'flourished in proportion to its bigness equal with any other in the university'. He added by way of explanation that 'this was effected by means of the exercise of a strict, even, and regular discipline'.

The close, almost fatherly relations Tullie maintained with his charges come vividly to light in the letters which John Freind, a lad of 17 who died in 1673 at the end of his first year, regularly sent to his father in Gloucestershire, who afterwards transcribed them.[8] It was the doctor's habit to visit 'the schollers chambers . . . almost every day to observe whether they followed their studyes'; once he surprised John in tears because 'I have bene with my Tutor and my Lecture is too hard for mee', and was able to cheer him up. From his careful accounts we learn that John's expenses in hall for the year amounted in all to £18. 16s. 0d; his total outlay, including

---

[6] See above pp. 38f. For 'Airay's' or 'Link Lodging' see *SEHM* (1925), 18–21.

[7] Bodleian Library, Tanner MS 454, fo. 142[r-v].

[8] *Memorialls and Remaines*, by Nathaniell Freind (Bodleian Library MS Top Oxon, fo. 31[r-v]).

books, clothes, journeys to and from home, tips, and all incidentals came to £37. 6s. 4d. Among the incidentals he enumerated certain 'unnecessary expences' amounting to 5s. 4d.—items such as 'oranges twice, 4d.', 'apples severall times and coffee, 5d.', 'milkhouse 3 times, 7½d.', 'at a pyehouse, 4d.', and 'seeing a shew, 4d'. His fellow scholars were deeply affected by his early death; there was a fever epidemic in Oxford at the time. At his funeral in St Peter's (where a memorial brass to him adorns the west wall) they 'were pleased many of them to exercise their Fancyes and to shew their love to him' by penning verses and fastening the sheets on which they were written to his hearse cloth.

Tullie was greatly helped by an able, conscientious vice-principal, John March, who had previously been a pupil of his at Queen's. John Friend's father came across March's 'method of studying' pasted up on the wall of his son's room, where he might have it always in view. Among other innovations Tullie started the custom whereby commoners of higher social rank were expected to present a piece of plate or a sum of money for the purchase of books on going down. He was also able to turn his Wiltshire connection to good effect. Through it he was able to influence five families in the county to send sons to the hall who later served as members of parliament. The best known of these was the John Methuen who, as well as representing Devizes from 1690 until his death, became lord chancellor of Ireland in 1697, and as ambassador to Portugal negotiated (1703) the trade treaty under which Portugal allowed the import, hitherto prohibited, of British woollen goods, while Britain agreed to levy on Portuguese wines a duty one-third less than on French wines.

II

Tullie had friends in high places, notably Sir Joseph Williamson, secretary of state from 1674, a fellow of Queen's and great benefactor of the college, but also Lord Crewe, bishop of Durham. Together these two secured him promotion at last, and in April 1675 he was appointed dean of Ripon. He was already broken in health, however, and died at Grittleton in mid-January 1676 before setting eyes on his cathedral.

To succeed him Queen's on 15 February elected Stephen Penton, BD, a former fellow of New College who was then rector of

4. The hall in 1675, from David Loggan's *Oxonia Illustrata*

45

Tingewick, near Buckingham, a New College living. Although the background of the transaction remains obscure, Queen's quite properly insisted that he should resign his benefice and that New College should then nominate a fellow of Queen's in his place; this it did within weeks. Author of a curious guide to the education of gentlemen's sons, Penton was praised by Thomas Hearne as 'a truly Honest, good Man, and an Excellent Scholar, and of so good and facetious a temper (without reserve) that he was beloved by all that knew him'. On the other hand, Andrew Allam, his vice-principal, considered[9] him a less capable administrator than Tullie, liking to indulge in experiments and gimmicks. Admissions certainly declined gradually during his principalship, from twenty-two in 1676 to eleven in 1680. In his last year they dropped to four, while the total membership of the hall fell to less than half what it had been in Tullie's time. One reason for this, Allam complained, was his marked preference for 'an inconsiderable set of gentlemen commoners, now his only darling creatures', in contrast to Tullie's readiness to accept young men of every social rank. In his defence, however, it should be noted that admissions were falling at other halls too at this time.

Penton's signal achievement was to complete the east end of the quadrangle by building what remains the hall's most ornate and distinctive architectural feature. Making a start in April 1680, on a strip of land granted by his former colleagues at New College for a nominal rent of one shilling a year, he erected the chapel and library in an ingeniously conjoint building.[10] This addition was a proud token of his society's prosperity and confidence, for of the other halls only Magdalen Hall had previously possessed a library (1657) and St Mary Hall a chapel (1642). To defray the cost he himself contributed generously from his own fortune; nor had he any qualms about selling all the silver plate, thirty-nine pieces in all, which had been given to the hall as leaving-presents under Tullie's rule. A sum of over £500 was also contributed by past and present members, by Queen's and its provost, Dr Timothy Halton (vice-chancellor at the time), and other well-wishers, and by Winchester College, where Penton had had his schooling. Even so, he had difficulty in raising the funds required. The mason builder

---

[9] Bodleian Library, Tanner MS 454, fo. 142^{r-v}.

[10] For a full description see A. B. Emden, *An Account of the Chapel and Library Building, St Edmund Hall, Oxford* (Oxford, 1932).

(architect too, probably) was Bartholomew Peisley; the design was obviously inspired by the English adaptations of the Palladian style which were setting the trend in Oxford, as exemplified, notably, by Christopher Wren's Sheldonian Theatre (built 1664–9) and, closer at hand, by the new north-east range of Queen's (completed 1672), which Sir Joseph Williamson had planned and financed.

The foundation-stone had been laid on 19 April 1680, and the chapel was consecrated, before the completion of the main building, on 7 April 1682 by Dr Fell, bishop of Oxford, with the title 'St Edmund's Chapel in the university of Oxford'. All the woodwork, including the oak screen and cedar wainscoting in the chapel and the cedar shelving in the library, was executed by Arthur Frogley, a then fashionable Oxford joiner (see, for example, his work in Trinity College chapel), all of it with the exception of the screen in 1688–90 after Penton's retirement. The library above, running transversely over the antechapel, was the first in Oxford to have the bookcases placed against the walls from floor to ceiling, with a gallery to provide access to the higher levels. It was the last Oxford library to have the books secured by chains (removed c.1760). It should be noted that, as originally constructed, the imposing façade looking west was in part a sham, for the upper and lower windows at the north end, with the portion of pediment above them, were blind dummies masking what was in fact a simple partition wall separating the north-east corner of the court from New College garden. This deception was maintained, as we shall see,[11] until 1931, when the library was extended northwards to its present size.

III

Penton's object in this ambitious undertaking was clearly to take his hall up market, opening it to sons of the gentry, possibly even of the nobility. If he had a few successes (seven of his eleven freshmen in 1681–2 were gentlemen commoners), they were short-lived. The hall was never to become the upper-class preserve he may have dreamed of, but for the next 250 years was to attract, like the other halls, mainly young men of modest means seeking an economical education. He resigned for health reasons on 7 March 1684,

---

[11] See below p. 117.

moving first to Glympton vicarage, Oxfordshire, and then in 1698 to Wath rectory, near Ripon, where he died in 1706. Meanwhile, eight days after his resignation, Queen's had elected its senior fellow, Dr Thomas Crosthwaite, who was admitted to office on 4 April. The sole relic of his brief reign is 'the New Leiger book'[12] which he started; it notes that all accounts with his predecessor had been squared on 21 March by the vice-principal and other masters in residence. On 30 October the vice-chancellor pronounced his appointment void; apparently he had insisted on retaining his fellowship, but the pretext advanced for ousting him was his dilatoriness in making the declaration, required of heads of houses under the act of uniformity (1662), repudiating the lawfulness of taking up arms against the crown. Although he was re-elected by a majority of Queen's fellows on 8 November, the provost (Timothy Halton), who was then at loggerheads with them, prevailed on the vice-chancellor to uphold his deprivation.[13] There followed months of wrangling, with an appeal to the visitor (the archbishop of York), but before he gave his ruling the college reached an accommodation, and on 5 May 1685 elected Dr John Mill, a former fellow who was then rector of Bletchingdon, Oxfordshire. Even so the matter was not settled, for Crosthwaite appealed to the queen as patroness of the college, and the provost and Mill had to go up to London.[14] Their visit must have been successful, for we hear no more of opposition.

In Mill the hall received one of the most learned, perhaps the most learned, of its principals. Humbly born at Shap in 1645, he entered Queen's at 16 as a 'poor boy', and as a recent graduate was chosen to speak the panegyric at the opening of the Sheldonian Theatre in 1669; he must already have 'talk'd and writ the best Latine of any man in the University'.[15] Elected a fellow in 1670, he rose to senior bursar, but in 1681, having uneasy relations with the provost, accepted the nearby rectory of Bletchingdon. About the same time, although only in his mid-thirties, he was appointed chaplain-in-ordinary to Charles II; he was to continue a royal chaplain during the next three reigns. He was so well thought of as a tutor that, when Queen's admitted the teenage prodigy Edmund

---

[12] Kept in the college archives.
[13] See T. Hearne, *Collections*, i. 306; ii. 280.
[14] Cf. J. R. Magrath, *The Flemings in Oxford* (Oxford, 1903–23), ii. 152.
[15] So White Kennett: see British Library MS Lansdowne 987, fo. 187ʳ⁻ᵛ.

Gibson (later bishop of London) in 1686, it broke with precedent and sent him across the lane for Mill to supervise him. The ablest of his vice-principals, White Kennett, noted[16] that he 'was the most aiery and facetious in Conversation, in all respects a bright man'; but he was also opinionated, with a violently abusive tongue. Hearne could be hard on him: 'a man of bad principles, and never failed to vent them'.[17] But such comments were politically motivated; he could never abide Mill's easygoing flexibility which led some to nickname him 'Johnny Windmill'. Politics apart, Hearne had a deep regard for Mill, and time and again cited his opinions of books or learned men with respect.

Although many found him disagreeable, Mill was a friend to scholars and an outstanding scholar himself. It was he, for example, who first noticed the genius of Richard Bentley, later to become a towering classical scholar, and spurred him on to prepare the work (in fact, his 'Epistle to Mill') which first established his reputation. He was active, too in fostering Anglo-Saxon studies in the university. His own great literary achievement, which brought him international renown and would have brought him the preferment he dreamed of had he lived longer, was his critical edition of the Greek New Testament. Published by the university press in 1707, he had worked on it from his days at Queen's for some thirty years, using student assistants to help him with collations and transcriptions. Although the text printed was that of Robert Estienne (1550), the prolegomena and apparatus were strikingly innovative, listing more than 30,000 variant readings, deploying an unprecedented number of manuscripts, and reviewing comprehensively the patristic citations. It was a masterpiece which was far ahead of its time, a creative landmark in the development of scientific New Testament criticism.[18]

It fell to Mill to finish the wainscoting of Penton's chapel, and to provide the gallery and shelving of the library and a tortuous staircase up to it. He also equipped the lodgings with wainscoting. The 'New Leiger book', which he had taken over, notes that the work on the lodgings cost £37. 18s. 9d., that on the library £39. 15s. od. From benefactors he obtained a handsome silver-gilt chalice and paten in 1688, and a flagon to match in 1692 (all still in

---

[16] See above n. 15.   [17] T. Hearne, *Collections*, iii. 21.
[18] For an analysis and assessment of it, as well as much information about Mill himself, see A. Fox, *John Mill and Richard Bentley* (Oxford, 1954).

5. Dr John Mill (from the portrait in The Queen's College)

occasional use). The Leiger book is crowded with fascinating items from his time, ranging from methodical accounts of the dues he received quarterly to 'charity money' occasionally disbursed—for example, to 'the poor woman that washes the dishes 2s.', 'a poor French Protestant 2s.', 'a disbanded officer of Ireland 10s.', 'a poor captive 6d.'. At five-yearly intervals Mill's dues are shown as amounting to £54. 10s. 11d. in 1685, £90. 11s. 10d. in 1690, £90. 18s. 0d. in 1695, £88. 8s. 0½d. in 1700, and £68. 13s. 2d. in 1705. An often overlooked entry near the beginning of the book records an agreement between Mill and the resident masters, dated 31 March 1686, on the scale of fees to be charged to an undergraduate on entrance and to graduates on taking their degrees. It suggests that, in spite of the principal's autocracy, the hall's masters were entitled to at least a measure of consultation.

Under Mill's rule the hall seems, until the turn of the century at any rate, to have been well thought of. When Sir Daniel Fleming, a substantial landowner in Westmorland, wrote to him in 1688 to introduce his son George, he dwelt[19] flatterously on 'the good report' he had received 'of the discipline of your Hall'; and Hearne confirms[20] that Mill took pride in the discipline he maintained. One example of his strictness was his transfer of evening prayer from between 5 and 6 p.m. to 9 p.m.; he made the change, according to Hearne,[21] 'on purpose to see People within'. Another was his abolition of the celebratory supper to which members of the hall taking their MA degree customarily subscribed; instead, he required them to contribute 20 shillings towards the purchase of books for the library, over and above the gift of 20 shillings to the library which Tullie had demanded of men going down. But, while approving of discipline, Hearne was quick to complain[22] when Mill, in a fit of temper, once sought to impose it on the masters of arts of the hall, summarily withdrawing from them their customary right to fine or otherwise punish impudent or negligent servants; he was only trying to ensure that nothing should be done 'but at the Pleasure and will of the Principal'.

Young George Fleming joined the hall in July 1688, taking his BA in 1692 but staying on until 1699; his letters home reveal[23] his

[19] J. R. Magrath, *The Flemings in Oxford*, ii. 212.
[20] T. Hearne, *Collections*, i. 141.   [21] Ibid. viii. 41.   [22] Ibid. i. 238.
[23] For this paragraph see J. R. Magrath, *The Flemings in Oxford*, iii. 310, 316; ii. 217, 252, 257, 262, 296; iii. 33.

affection for it and for Mill. When his younger brother James made a mess of things at Queen's (the Flemings were a Queen's family), he pressed his father to transfer him to the hall, which he would find much stricter and more economical. He himself kept accounts of all his expenses in fascinating detail, noting not only room-rent, tuition fees, books, and the like, but such items as paper, candles, chamber-pots. In his first year his outgoings amounted to £34. 12s. 11d., and during the following three rose by about £10 yearly. Once settled in he reports having daily lectures in logic with the vice-principal, 'Mr Codrington, who is very sober, civil, diligent, and a laborious man'. In May 1689 he describes how busy he is with moral philosophy; he has 'Disputations, Declamations, Recitations, and other exercise constantly'. But his interest has switched to 'the Common Law, as being that which I alwayes even from my childhood, but now much more admire.' However, his father was firm: 'Whilst you shall continue in the University, I would have your cheif Study to be Logick, Ethicks, Phisicks, Metaphisicks, and Divinity.' This last would be best for body and soul, and might well lead to a good living, whereas to be a lawyer would call for expensive years at the inns of court. The letters are full of references to Mill and his numerous kindnesses to the young man. One summer, when smallpox was rife in Oxford and most people had fled to the country, only Mill and he were left in the hall: 'he took the trouble severall times upon him, to come to my Chamber and to see what I was doing, and to look what sorts of bookes I had gotten.' George once described him to his father as 'my greatest friend next your self'.

Yet Mill's firm hold on his vigorous little society seems to have slackened as his absorption in his New Testament researches grew steadily intenser. He also continued rector of Bletchingdon, eight miles away, until his death, and he did regular turns of duty in London as royal chaplain; in 1705 he was appointed to a lucrative prebendal stall at Canterbury. White Kennett, who was vice-principal 1691–5, complained[24] that he 'was so much taken up with the One Thing his Testament that he had not leisure to attend to the Discipline of the House, which rose and fell according to his different Vice-Principals.' Hearne noted[25] that, when Kennett left the hall, several of its junior members seized the opportunity to

---

[24] British Library MS Lansdowne 987, fo. 187ʳ⁻ᵛ.
[25] T. Hearne, *Collections*, i. 117.

migrate to Lincoln College. He also criticized[26] Mill for taking 'successively three Vice-Principals from other places . . . when there were several of the Hall who would have accepted of it' and done well in the office. Whatever the reason for his high-handed policy, it is evident that the hall suffered a steep decline in numbers (reflected, as we have seen, in his dues) in his last decade as principal. In 1688, when George Fleming was entered, there were ten matriculations, but this number was never again reached. In the span 1700 to 1707 yearly matriculations averaged less than five. In the month in which he died in the latter year Hearne wrote[27] to an old member describing the hall as 'not very full'.

IV

With its reputation standing high, with its new dining-hall and stately chapel-library, and with principals like Tullie and Mill presiding over it, the hall was enjoying a golden period during the years covered by this chapter. Never before, and never since until quite recent times, could it count among its alumni so many gifted people destined to make a mark in scholarship, the arts, or public life. Among those admitted by Tullie we can point (in addition to the MPs already named) two future speakers of the house of commons, Sir Thomas Littleton and Sir Richard (later baron) Onslow; to a prominent physician and much abused poet, Sir Richard Blackmore; and to two writers who won plaudits in widely different circles, the brilliant satiric poet John Oldham, and John Kettlewell, the non juring devotional author. One of Penton's gentlemen commoners was Francis Cherry of Shottesbrooke, Berkshire, collector of books and coins, friend of the saintly bishop Ken and like him a non-juror. Mill's scholars included not only his favourite, George Fleming, who, in spite of the earlier 'innate avertion I naturally had to holy orders', rose to be a 'civilized but wholly unenthusiastic' bishop of Carlisle, but also White Kennett and (until he was lured away to University College) Humphrey Wanley. Kennett, who served Mill loyally but critically as vice-principal for five years, was to be the father of parish history and a scholarly bishop of Peterborough, Wanley a renowned

---

[26] Ibid. i. 141.
[27] Bodleian Library MS Rawlinson Letters 36, fo. 300^{r-v}.

6. Thomas Hearne, holding a volume inscribed with his personal motto (*suum cuique*—'to each his own')

palaeographer, librarian, and pioneer of Anglo-Saxon studies at a time when Oxford was their vital centre.

Another remarkable character who was admitted by Mill but long outlived him was Thomas Hearne, whose voluminous, caustic, but always informative diaries provide a rich kaleidoscope for thirty years of Oxford personalities and happenings. He has already appeared in these pages, but this is the place to sketch him a little more fully. A Berkshire lad of humble parentage, he was sent to the hall in 1695 by his local squire, no other than Francis Cherry of Shottesbrooke. Graduating BA in 1699, he rejected attractive invitations to leave Oxford, preferring to work his way up in the Bodleian Library. Starting as a janitor, he became deputy librarian, and did valuable work indexing and cataloguing its collections. At Mill's instigation he also made the earliest catalogue of the hall's library, listing 421 volumes. Like his patron Cherry, however, Hearne was an intransigent adherent of the Stuart house, and steadfastly refused to take the oath of allegiance to the Hanoverian George I which was required of all university officers. For this he was deprived of his position in Bodley, as also of his membership of the university, in 1716.

Through the kindness of Mill's successor, Dr Thomas Pearson, he was allowed to retain his rooms in the hall, although his name could not appear in the buttery-book. From c.1707, probably, these consisted of a superior double set on Staircase 1, with windows overlooking both the churchyard and the quadrangle, on the first floor over what was then the buttery.[28] From them, although excluded from libraries, he continued to edit and publish pioneer, but still remarkably accurate, editions of medieval chroniclers and other source-material of English history, earning from them a comfortable living. He also carried on a vast correspondence with antiquaries and librarians, while from 1705 to within a few days of his death he was jotting down every detail of Oxford life and gossip that came his way in the 140 notebooks of his diary. When he died, in 1735, he was buried in the north-east section of St Peter's churchyard, where his tomb with the inscription (restored) 'who studied and preserved antiquities' can still be seen. A devout man, he left a characteristic prayer in which, after praising God for his singular providence, he gave thanks 'in a particular manner' for having been guided to the discovery of three hitherto unknown manuscripts.

[28] For their identification see A. B. Emden in *SEHM* (1920–1), 22–8. For their remodelling as a room bearing his name see below, p. 117.

VI

Stand-Still, Revival, Witch-Hunt

I

JOHN MILL died of a stroke on 23 June 1707, exactly a fortnight after the publication of his epoch-making Greek New Testament. We are better informed about his death than about any event in his life, for it was described at length in letters[1] by archdeacon Worth, one of his great friends, and Thomas Hearne, both of whom were praying at his bedside. While detesting his Whiggism, and noting (for example) that his lodgings alone in Oxford were lit up in celebration of Marlborough's victories, Hearne freely admitted that he had been a friend, and bore 'the Character of a Learned Divine, a charitable man to the Poor, and in several respects of a Publick Spirit'. He had intended, Hearne relates, to make a substantial bequest to the hall, but as he died intestate nothing came of this. He had, however, left the hall so 'thin' in numbers that none of the fellows of Queen's would accept the principalship unless the college made an advantageous arrangement with him. When therefore it elected Thomas Pearson, DD, in August 1707, it was obliged to agree that he should have a comfortable benefice as soon as one fell vacant, and pending that should be provided with 'a pension . . . equivalent to a Fellowship' (a deal which Hearne deplored as entirely unconstitutional).[2] In the event, having been instituted by the vice-chancellor on 9 August, he was next year installed as vicar of Sulhampstead Abbots, Berkshire, a college living.

Hearne evidently approved of Pearson, 'a modest, good natur'd Man, and a plain practical Preacher'. His approval was politically motivated: he was pleased to note that, when George I ascended the throne, Pearson absented himself from the meeting of convocation

---

[1] Lambeth MS 933, art. 42 (repr. in the *Gentleman's Magazine*, 71, p. 587); Bodleian Library MS Rawlinson Letters 37, fo. 134^{r-v}.

[2] T. Hearne, *Collections*, ii. 22 (his estimate of Mill); i. 10, 34 (lodgings illuminated); ii. 32 (Pearson's election).

which voted a loyal address to the new Hanoverian king. The esteem seems to have been mutual, for (as already recorded) Pearson allowed Hearne to retain his rooms in hall when he forfeited his offices in the university. Little or nothing, however, is known about his principalship (1707–22), except that he did nothing to arrest the decline which had set in during Mill's later years. Matriculations only once, in 1715, reached five; in several years there was none at all. This contrasted with a flourishing intake at, for example, Hart Hall and Magdalen Hall, and with a slight increase in university admissions generally. To some extent ill health was probably to blame, for in his last five or six years he was confined to his vicarage near Reading in 'a miserable condition', afflicted with 'the dead Palsey'. He died there, 'a very poor man', on 15 February 1722.[3]

Things did not improve, but rather worsened, under his successor. This was Henry Felton, DD, a graduate of the hall who had migrated to Queen's and then moved to London, where he had acquired a reputation as a fashionable preacher. His volumes attacking Roman Catholics and Protestants who deviated from the Thirty-Nine Articles, and also his superficial but readable *Dissertation on Reading the Classics and Forming a Just Style*, ran to several printings. Hearne dismissed the last, which he typically dedicated to a former pupil, the Marquis of Granby, as 'a meer injudicious Rhapsody'.[4] Queen's, which elected him on 19 April 1722, was not called upon to give him a benefice; as chaplain to three successive dukes of Rutland, he had been presented by them to one in Derbyshire in 1712, and then in 1736 given Barwick, Yorkshire. Hearne regarded him as pretentious and self-opinionated ('a poor, vain, halfstrained, conceited man'), and others seem to have shared his assessment. In particular, he criticized him for shifting the time of evening prayers back from 9 to 5 p.m. (which left the young men free to roam the town), and that of dinner forward from 11 a.m. to 12 noon, for reinstating the supper which pious tradition had hitherto omitted on Fridays, and for dispensing with the serving of pancakes at dinner on Shrove Tuesday: 'when laudable old Customs alter, 'tis a Sign Learning dwindles'.[5]

Numbers at the hall continued 'thin', matriculations being even fewer than under Pearson. There was none at all in four of Felton's

---

[3] Ibid. vii. 331.   [4] Ibid. ix. 63.   [5] Ibid. ix. 373; viii. 41, 69, 50.

last years, but he should not necessarily be blamed for this. Admissions were now steadily falling in the colleges and halls generally; the intake at Magdalen Hall, for example, was more than halved in the decade 1730–9. More to be questioned was his resort to accepting migrants from other societies, sometimes men who had not been furnished with the customary leaving certificates or who had even been expelled. The new vice-principal he installed, James Creed, a young graduate from Queen's, seems also to have been thoroughly unsatisfactory; Hearne jeered at him for preaching the Latin sermon 'purely to get a little money to spend upon Girls', and for being 'much given to Women (taking as little care of the Hall as . . . the Principal).[6] As for Felton himself, Hearne complained[7] that he was allowing 'all manner of litterary Discipline fall down at Edmund Hall'). Yet Felton had ambitions for his small society, and in 1727 began seriously planning the reconstruction of the dilapidated north range of the quadrangle. One November morning Hearne caught sight of him, in both the quadrangle and the churchyard, having measurements taken 'in order to make a Draught for a new building'; he was saying 'that the Hall (at least the North side) shall speedily (by his care) be new built'.[8] The project came to nothing (it was probably an example of his pretentiousness), but if he had succeeded in carrying it out, he would have replaced the existing domestic Gothic buildings with imposing Palladian ones reminiscent of Queen's. His dreams survive in an elaborate plan of the redesigned north façade which William Williams hopefully included in his *Oxonia depicta* (1732–3), a splendid volume to which Felton himself subscribed.

II

These years of stand-still, not to say set-back, were followed by a decade of revived activity. As successor to Felton, who died at Barwick on 1 March 1740, Queen's appointed one of its ablest fellows, Thomas Shaw, DD, a man of robust and vigorous, even pugnacious personality and exceptionally wide experience and scholarship.[9] A native of Kendal, he had taken his degree through Queen's, and had spent thirteen years as chaplain to the English merchant community at Algiers. Using this as his base, he made a series of adventurous expeditions to Egypt and Palestine, including

---

[6] T. Hearne, *Collections*, viii. 320; ix. 69.
[7] Ibid. viii. 94.   [8] Ibid. ix. 373.   [9] See *DNB*.

Jerusalem, as well as 'in the interior of Barbary', i.e. Algeria, Morocco, Tunisia, and Libya, amassing a vast range of scientific and archaeological material as he travelled. He had been elected a fellow of Queen's in his absence, and on his return in 1737 it was characteristic of him to demand that a decision taken while he was still abroad should be reconsidered. About the same time he was elected a fellow of the Royal Society (the hall's second FRS), to whose transactions he had contributed a geographical description of the kingdom of Tunis in 1729. His *Travels or Observations relating to several parts of Barbary and the Levant*, published in a sumptuously illustrated folio in 1738 and listing 640 species of plants, at once won him acclaim as a naturalist; before long it was translated into French, Dutch, and German. At Oxford he was nominated regius professor of Greek, while Queen's presented him (1742) to the vicarage of Bramley, Hampshire; he was the first of seven successive principals to hold this valuable benefice in conjunction with their office.

Shaw had three vice-principals in succession. The first, Thomas Camplin, a Queen's man, was something of an amateur architect, and designed the Holywell Music Room;[10] he subsequently became archdeacon of Bath. The second (1747), Jonathan Edwards, had been bursar of Magdalen Hall but had left owing to a dispute with his principal.[11] The third, John Higson, whom he appointed a few months before his death, formerly of Wadham, was an unbalanced character of whom we shall hear more. With the help of the first two Shaw threw himself energetically into his new work, and succeeded in reversing the decline in numbers, doubling the intake at a time when admissions to the university at large were continuing to fall steeply. His great achievement, however, was the complete reconstruction and refurbishment of the buildings, which on coming to the hall he found[12] 'in a ruinous Condition; occasioned as well from length of Time, as for the want of proper Repairs, whenever they became necessary'.

First, he thoroughly repaired the chapel, refectory, lodgings, and the eastern half of the north range. He then (*c.*1746) demolished the larger, western half of the north range which, 'having been built

---

[10] See J. H. Mee, *The Oldest Music Room in Europe* (London, 1911), 7.
[11] See his pamphlet, *The Substance of two Actions and the Proceeding therein, in the University Court of Oxford* (Oxford, 1749).
[12] Cf. his appeal, printed in part, VCH, 324*b*.

7. Thomas Shaw, DD, FRS. 'His countenance is described as "grotesque, but marked most strongly with jocularity and good humour" ' (*DNB*)

more than 400 years agoe, was ready to drop down, and not capable of being repaired; as all the old materials were found, upon Examination, to be rotten and decayed'. He then rebuilt it from the foundations, raising it by an additional storey with attics so that its elevation matched that of the eastern sector. The sole relic of the medieval structure which he retained was the ancient kitchen fireplace, now a feature of the lower buttery. At the junction of the north range he fixed a sundial, originally black-and-white, but painted in brilliant colours with a Latin epigram in 1952 in commemoration of the ~~coronation~~ *accession* of Elizabeth II.[13] To finance all these constructional works he did not hesitate to dig deeply into his own pocket, spending (he claimed)[14] more than £400; he also issued an appeal and enlisted supporters from outside the hall whose names are preserved in the *Book of Benefactors, 1659–1861*. He died on 15 August 1751 at Bramley, where the inscription on his tomb salutes him as the 'munificent restorer' of his hall.

III

Little is known about the hall's fortunes under Shaw's successor, George Fothergill, DD, whom Queen's elected on 19 October 1752, except that matriculations began to fall again; indeed, there was none at all in two of his nine years. It is not surprising that he made little impact, for he seems to have regarded the principalship as a stepping-stone to the provostship of Queen's, on which he had set his heart. Of yeoman stock from Ravenstonedale, on the borders of Westmorland and Yorkshire, he had worked his way through the college in the humble role of servitor; a vivid picture of the tasks he had to perform, and of the money he earned, in that capacity is provided in his letters to his parents.[15] With six other servitors he had to 'wait upon the Batchelors, Gent. Commoners and Commoners at meals. We carry in their Commons out of the Kitchen into the Hall, and their bread and beer out of the Buttery.' He also had to 'call up' three commoners and one gentleman commoner in the morning; he calculated that all these duties 'will save me about eight pounds a year one way or other'.

[13] See *SEHM* (1953), 12–13.
[14] See *VCH*, 24*b*.
[15] See C. Thornton and F. McLaughlin, *The Fothergills of Ravenstonedale* (London, 1905).

In 1734 he had been rewarded with a fellowship; he at once wrote home requesting his parents, 'if it can be done without ostentation', to call all his relations and spend half a crown, or perhaps more, in entertaining them. As dean, however, he had brought the college embarrassing notoriety in 1748 by his clumsy mishandling of an undergraduate boycott of hall dinner because of allegedly unappetizing boiled beef.[16] In spite of this he stood for the provostship in 1756, when he was now installed at the hall, but narrowly missed election; in fact, he tied with his rival, who was eventually chosen, as the statutes required, on the ground that he was senior of the two. Always unsure of himself, blundering and pedantic, and plagued with ill health, the legacy perhaps of the deprivations of his early years, he died on 30 October 1760 at the age of 54. He was the first principal to be buried in the chapel.

IV

In Fothergill's place Queen's appointed another fellow of the college, George Dixon, DD, presenting him also to Bramley vicarage. He must have been the first principal to look out across the lane from his lodgings, no longer on the crumbling, 400-years-old Gothic gatehouse of Queen's, but on the newly completed (1757–61), stiffly monotonous east-facing façade of Hawksmoor's magnificent front quadrangle. Neither he nor any of his colleagues could have foreseen, when he took up residence there, the storm that was to shake the hall to its foundations before many years had passed.

Prior to his election as a fellow in 1748, Dixon had worked as a parish priest and preacher, mainly in London, preferring 'the labours of a parochial ministry to the indolent or even literary retirement of a college'.[17] He was in fact a profoundly spiritual man who, as an undergraduate at Queen's in 1729–34, had had links with members of the Holy Club which the brothers John and Charles Wesley had started in 1729 to foster individual piety among university men, and which had some disciples in the college. He also had useful connections, so that under him admissions

---

[16] For the extraordinary affair see J. R. Magrath, *The Queen's College*, ii. 111, 207–36 (documents).

[17] So his obituarist in *Gentleman's Magazine*, 57, pp. 287–8.

began to revive (there were as many as ten in 1766), and numbers at the hall, which had recently averaged around a dozen, showed signs of a modest increase. Several of those he accepted were earnest evangelicals, some of them allegedly sponsored by Selina, countess of Huntingdon (1707–91), the devout foundress of the Calvinistic Methodist chapels known as her 'Connexion', whose friendship he valued and with whose views he was inclined to sympathize. Some of these young men got into the habit of foregathering on Sunday evenings, for Bible-study and extempore prayer, at the house of Mrs Durbridge, pious widow of a sadler of the town and herself a convert of George Whitefield. Two or three were even rumoured to preach on occasion at Methodist conventicles. Dixon was not unduly alarmed; as his obituarist remarked, he was ready 'to esteem religion wherever he found it, and to excuse errors and imperfections where he thought he discovered truth'.

The vice-principal, John Higson (he had held the office since Shaw's last year), was not disposed to be so charitable. A deeply prejudiced man, with a streak of insanity in his make-up, he was furious that the hall was beginning to lie under the odium 'of there being too much religion there'.[18] His protests against the admission of palpable Methodists left Dixon unmoved; he did, however, encourage Higson to put on lectures on the Thirty-Nine Articles 'that he might satisfy himself whether they held any erroneous opinions'. This he did at 9 p.m., leading one man to object that it was 'like being sent to the Gallies'; but he was able to convince himself that some of the men held extreme Calvinistic views on doctrines like election and grace. But when he complained to the principal that 'there were several Enthusiasts' at the hall 'who talked of regeneration, inspiration, and drawing nigh to God', he met with the tart rejoinder that 'these were all scriptural expressions, and the use of them authorized by the offices of the Church of England.' He therefore took the matter into his own hands, and on 29 February 1768 delated the seven young men he deemed guilty to the vice-chancellor as visitor of the hall, with a view to having their suspected Methodist affiliations investigated. Dixon lost his temper, and threatened to dismiss him; but Higson got an assurance from the provost of Queen's that this could not be done without the vice-chancellor's express permission.

[18] R. Hill, *Goliath Slain* (London, 1768), 187.

Meanwhile, the trial of the students went ahead, and on 11 March they were brought before the vice-chancellor (Dr Durell, principal of Hertford), sitting with four assessors and the university registrar in the hall refectory, in the presence of a vast and vociferously hostile crowd of gownsmen. A medley of charges was brought against them—academic insufficiency and even illiteracy, lack of deference to their tutor (Higson himself), even (in the case of three of them) having been brought up to trade: there were distinct overtones of class prejudice in the affair. Their real offence, however, in the eyes of their accusers, was dabbing in Methodism, uncritically assumed to be inimical to the doctrine and discipline of the established church. Dixon testified manfully to their orthodoxy, as also to their high personal character; but in spite of the flimsy and ill-assorted evidence adduced the verdict, solemnly delivered later in the day in the chapel, went against them. Six of the seven (the charges against one had been dropped on the grounds that he was a man of fortune and not a candidate for holy orders) were found guilty and sentenced to expulsion both from the hall and from the university. Higson was commended for his public spirit in bringing the matter to the attention of the authorities.[19]

V

The incident sparked off a lively pamphlet war, both within and outside Oxford. A champion of the six students sarcastically inquired whether, even granting they had all been present at prayer-meetings in Mrs Durbridge's house, that was to be regarded as more harmful than, for example, had they been lounging for hours on end at billiard-tables or on tennis-courts. George Whitefield, the famous Methodist orator and evangelist, wrote to the vice-chancellor suggesting that, if it was disgraceful for ordinands to be caught singing hymns, praying extempore, and expounding verses of scripture, the question in the ordination service, 'Do you trust that you are inwardly moved by the Holy Ghost?' should surely be amended to, 'Do you trust that you are NOT moved by the Holy Ghost?' But it was Dr Johnson's comment which best reflected the

[19] See S. L. Ollard, *The Six Students of St Edmund Hall* (Oxford, 1911); also V. H. H. Green in, *History of the University of Oxford* (Oxford, 1986), v. 458–64. A fundamental source is Bodleian Library MS St Edmund Hall 56 (the Higson papers).

complacency of the establishment, obdurately insensitive to the growing disquiet at its tyrannical hold over education in the universities. The expulsion, he remarked,[20] 'was extremely just and proper. What have they to do at a University, who are not willing to be taught, but will presume to teach?' When Boswell protested that it was surely hard to expel the young men, since they were said to be 'good beings', the doctor retorted, 'Sir, I believe they might be good beings; but they were not fit to be in the University of Oxford. A cow is a very good animal in the field; but we turn her out of a garden.'

For the hall the episode, which had brought it unwelcome, nation-wide notoriety, was an embarrassment which could not but cause a set-back. There was a steep fall in admissions for the next decade, although university numbers were beginning to increase. Dixon himself had inevitably to face a sharp cut in his income as a result both of the expulsions themselves and of the decline in applications; what was perhaps worse, he had been publicly humiliated, and that at the instigation of his own vice-principal. Higson had of course to leave the hall immediately; he retired to the vicarage of Batheaston, Somerset, to which Christ Church (of which he had been a chaplain since 1754) had presented him in 1766. But with the university Dixon felt, understandably, that his relations had become distinctly uncomfortable. He could hardly expect preferment, however, and so he soldiered on as principal for nineteen years more, until his death on 8 March 1787.

It is intriguing that, notwithstanding all that had happened, he continued to admit young men of pronounced evangelical leanings to his hall. One such was Edward Spencer, whom he presented for matriculation only a few months later, on 11 June, already in holy orders and 28 years old. Intensely loyal to the established church, and also of gentle birth, Spencer had an undisturbed career at Oxford, and later, as rector of Wingfield, Wiltshire, exerted (as we shall see) a formative influence on zealous young men whom he took in as his pupils and indoctrinated. Another, admitted exactly a year after the expulsions, was Joseph Benson, also a mature student, a very able man who had been John Wesley's classics master at Kingswood. By contrast with Spencer, his unconcealed association with Wesley and Lady Huntingdon got him into

---

[20] *Boswell's Life of Johnson*, ed. G. B. Hill, rev. L. F. Powell (Oxford, 1934), ii. 187.

trouble, and the strict vice-principal, Edward Bowerbank, refused to sign the testimonial necessary for his ordination. As a result he went down degree-less, was lost to the church of England, but became one of the most famous Wesleyan Methodist preachers and writers.

VII

Evangelical Interlude

T H E long span, more than half a century, stretching from Principal Dixon's death to the report of the first royal commission on Oxford, saw a succession of four principals presiding over the hall. These were William Dowson, DD, admitted 13 October 1787, died 10 January 1800; George Thompson, DD, admitted 15 April 1800, died 16 May 1823; Anthony Grayson, DD, admitted 3 February 1824, died 6 September 1843; and William Thompson, DD, admitted 6 November 1843, died 15 September 1854. To complete the story two details should be added. First, on G. Thompson's death Queen's resolved to present Henry Wheatley, MA, 'to the Principality of Edmund Hall and to the vicarage of Bramley', but although instituted to the latter he died before being admitted to the former, and has therefore never been included in the list of principals. Secondly, when W. Thompson was instituted, the vice-principal (J. Hill), as he himself recalled in his diary, made a formal declaration in Latin to the vice-chancellor to the effect, 'In my own name and in that of this St Edmund Hall I assent to this nomination.' There was, so far as is known, no precedent for this, and its interpolation suggests that there was a growing feeling in aularian circles that, when a principal was appointed, something more than the mere fiat of Queen's, some measure perhaps of consultation, was called for.

All four principals were Queen's men and senior fellows of the college; all four were appointed to the vicarage of Bramley, but W. Thompson held it only briefly. While taking part in university business as heads of houses, all four were content to leave the day-to-day running of the hall, apart from presiding in chapel when in residence, to their vice-principals. But they expected to be consulted on serious matters, and clearly kept in touch with what was happening. There was an illuminating illustration of this in November 1821, when an undergraduate was found to be suffering from syphilis, and the shocked vice-principal (again Hill) decided he could do nothing until the principal, who was out of Oxford, returned. When he did a day or two later, he remarked that he was not surprised, for he had observed the company the young man kept. He then sentenced him to a year's rustication.

The shortness of W. Thompson's tenure of Bramley vicarage resulted from the maturing of a benefaction which materially strengthened the hall's position. Some eighty years previously, in June 1763, Dr George Holme, a former fellow of Queen's who had served as chaplain to the English merchants at Algiers, had bequeathed the sum of £1,000 to the university to be invested until, with the interest accruing, sufficient money had been accumulated to purchase the advowson of a living worth at least £200 a year; this, he stipulated, should be attached to the hall. In 1821 the university used the fund to acquire the rectory of Gatcombe, in the Isle of Wight, and when the living fell vacant in 1844 Thompson resigned from Bramley (it had been agreed at his election that he should do so at the first vacancy) and was appointed to it. From that date until 1917 the principals of the hall were to enjoy the emoluments of Gatcombe rectory. They resided in the parish periodically; it is not clear how often, but mostly in the vacations, although sometimes for short portions of full term. For the rest they discharged their pastoral duties through a curate whose modest stipend they defrayed.

II

Under these four principals the hall first threw off the stagnation of Dixon's latter years, and then embarked on an era marked, until near its close, by consolidation and steady growth. Matriculations, which had sunk to a trickle, revived remarkably. Reckoned by decades, they averaged five a year for 1790–9, nine a year for 1800–9, and about ten a year for 1810–19 and 1820–9. After that they fell back slightly, but stayed just below eight a year for 1830–9 and eight a year for 1840–9. In the late forties and early fifties, however, they were definitely slipping (only eight in all for the three years 1850–2). Although there were exceptions, those admitted were usually men of modest financial background, attracted by the hall's relative inexpensiveness. The great majority—almost 70 per cent in two sample years, 1818/19 and 1848/9, as against just under 50 per cent for Oxford as a whole[1]—were destined for holy orders.

One small but important extension to the buildings was taken in hand at the beginning of G. Thompson's principalship. In May 1800, shortly after his election, Queen's entered into an arrangement with him under which he was allowed, in return for £2. 2s. 6d. in respect of annual rent and ordinary fine, to take down a tenement adjoining the hall 'for the purpose of enlarging his dwelling-house'.[2] The demolition of this small house (which appears as it was in 1675 in D. Loggan's famous print of the hall) enabled him to construct a single-storey room (or rooms) on the site at present occupied by the dining-room of the principal's lodgings. At some subsequent date, which cannot be exactly determined but which (to judge by contemporary prints) must have been before 1832, a second storey was added.

The most noteworthy feature, however, of this period was the hall's identification during the whole of it with the evangelical revival then stirring in the church of England. For a time, indeed, from 1783 to 1812, it was effectively the headquarters of the movement in Oxford, and a later historian[3] of evangelicalism could describe it as 'the religion of Teddy Hall'. The initial impulse to this positively Protestant orientation had been given by Principal Dixon, who (as we noted in the previous chapter) continued quietly but with steady determination to recruit evangelically disposed undergraduates even after the expulsions of 1768. But the men really responsible were three remarkable, personally very different, vice-principals who successively impressed their own religious preferences on the small community: Isaac Crouch, 1783–1807; Daniel Wilson, 1807–12; and John Hill, 1812–51. All of them were graduates of the hall, and all of them were married when they held office and lived in houses which they rented in the town.

III

Much the most influential of the three was probably Crouch; indeed, his contribution to the evangelical revival in Oxford was

[1] I owe these figures to the kindness of Mark Curthoys.
[2] See J. R. Magrath, *The Queen's College*, ii. 150.
[3] G. R. Balleine, *A History of the Evangelical Party in the Church of England* (2nd edn., London, 1933), 133.

early compared[4] to that of his more famous contemporary, Charles Simeon (1759–1836), to its Cambridge counterpart. Humbly born at Bradford, he had been briefly the pupil of an earlier aularian evangelical, Edward Spencer,[5] and it was probably on his recommendation that he entered the hall in 1774. After he had served a couple of curacies, Dixon (again showing his predilection for evangelicals) invited him back in 1783 to become vice-principal. From then until his retirement in 1806 he was an exceptionally busy man, being not only effectively in charge of the hall, but riding out most Sundays to Chislehampton and Stadhampton, six miles south-east of Oxford, to take services for the absentee pluralist incumbent. He was much respected in the university, served several times as pro-proctor, and frequently occupied the pulpit of St Mary's.

A quiet, undemonstrative man of wide learning, Crouch lectured on the whole range of subjects (Hebrew, Greek, Latin, mathematics, French, natural philosophy) then studied at pass level by undergraduates. His own special interest was in church history, and he was said to have given the hall 'a novel character for erudition no less than seriousness'. But his chief concern was to deepen the evangelical commitment of his charges. He therefore lectured to them assiduously on the Greek New Testament, arranging that each student should cover it in its entirety during his course. In addition he conducted devotional reading-parties for small groups on Sunday evenings, and invited every junior member of the hall to dinner in his house once a term and to private sessions with himself two or three times a term. As the years went by, more and more earnest spirits were attracted to the hall by the reputation which his concerned supervision gave it. To cite but a single example, William Marsh, son of Colonel Sir Charles Marsh of Reading, later to become a celebrated preacher (nicknamed 'Millennial Marsh' because of his obsession with the millennium in his sermons), chose the hall in 1797 in preference to any other college 'on account of the Christian character and evangelical views of its Principal [sic], Dr [sic] Crouch, and several of its undergraduates . . .'.

---

[4] See his obituary in the *Christian Observer* (1837), 410–11.
[5] See above p. 65

8. Isaac Crouch, Vice-Principal 1783–1807

IV

Under its next vice-principal the hall continued to be the main centre of evangelicalism in Oxford, although it was no longer the only one and few of its junior members later rose to prominence in evangelical circles.[6] Daniel Wilson, son of a wealthy London silk manufacturer, had at first been apprenticed to the family business, but, on experiencing a conversion and feeling (much to his father's disgust) a call to the ministry, entered the hall in 1798. 'The society', his biographer[7] recalled, 'was but small, and, perhaps . . . better known for its piety than its learning.' It was probably its reputation for piety that had drawn him to it, and he soon formed an immense regard for his tutor, Isaac Crouch. Crouch fully reciprocated this, and when Wilson was serving his curacy at Chobham and Bisley summoned him back in 1804 with a view to his becoming assistant tutor. Wilson accepted, settled with his family in the High Street, and in 1807 succeeded Crouch as vice-principal and sole tutor. From 1804 to 1809 he was also curate of Upper and Nether Worton, villages lying between Banbury and Woodstock where his uncle was principal landowner. In the vacations his wife and he resided at Worton, but in term-time he would leave Oxford at 8 a.m. in a post-chaise, cover the sixteen miles to his parish, and there conduct the prescribed services and preach. Although the work was taxing, it was not unremunerative; his biographer records[8] that his tutorship and curacy together yielded 'about £500 per annum'.

Wilson was intellectually outstanding—'one of the most notable scholars who adorned the early Oxford Renascence'.[9] As tutor, however, he had no doubt that his 'main object must be so to instruct [his pupils] in the saving knowledge of God . . . that, however little they may profit by me in secular matters, they may nevertheless learn to love God, to believe in Christ . . . '.[10] In fact, he devoted himself energetically and efficiently to his secular tasks

---

[6] Cf. J. S. Reynolds, *The Evangelicals at Oxford, 1735–1871* (Oxford, 1953), 82.

[7] J. Bateman, *The Life of the Right Rev. Daniel Wilson, D.D.* (2nd edn., London, 1861), 27.

[8] Ibid. 76.

[9] W. Tuckwell, *Pre-Tractarian Oxford* (London, 1909), 5.

[10] From his diary: quoted by Bateman, *The Life of the Right Rev. Daniel Wilson, DD*, 66.

(as he liked to call them), which since the introduction of honour schools in 1801 now included preparing a few more ambitious or able men for both mathematical and classical honours. As a result of his efforts, the hall began to rank high in academic achievement. Like Crouch, he also had the habit of inviting undergraduates to meals with his wife and family at his home. Yet he found it difficult, stiff and donnish as he was, to unbend with them. A stickler for academic propriety, he reproved students who turned up in his drawing-room not wearing bands (at a time when their regular use had all but disappeared), and earned for himself the nickname 'Bands Wilson'. Even his biographer had to confess[11] that these evening parties 'wanted ease. The desire to do good was too obvious to be pleasant; and the family prayers which closed the evening were oftentimes personal and monitory.'

The fact is that, for all his ability and efficiency, his heart was not in his academic, or 'secular' work. 'My time at Oxford', he was to write many years later,[12] 'was utterly without profit as to my soul.' By contrast, he found complete spiritual satisfaction in ministering to the simple peasants of the Wortons, who thronged their little church enraptured by his preaching. In 1809 he accepted with relief (although it entailed a drop of £200 a year in his income) a call to become minister of St John's Chapel, Bedford Row, for the next three years spending the vacations and as much of the term as he could spare from his Oxford commitments in London. It was an unsatisfactory arrangement, but he had agreed with the principal (G. Thompson) to delegate most of his duties to his successor-designate, John Hill, while he himself retained general superintendence of the hall until Hill, who had just taken his BA, was ready to take over as vice-principal.[13]

After 1812 Wilson only saw Oxford as an occasional visitor. In 1817, for example, he preached a university sermon in which he argued that the regeneration obtained in baptism was not necessarily identical with regeneration in the full gospel sense. It gave great offence in Oxford, and the vice-chancellor forbade the university press to print it: 'it savours', he remarked, 'of St Edmund Hall'. From now onwards, however, he was embarked on a public career of ever-growing influence and distinction, becoming bishop of Calcutta and Anglican metropolitan of India in 1832. These

---

[11] Ibid. 67.   [12] Ibid.   [13] Ibid. 77.

roles gave ample scope to his missionary zeal, imperious determination, and considerable administrative capacity. Almost the only
facts regarding St Edmund Hall deemed worthy of mention in the
Victorian edition of Karl Baedeker's *Great Britain* were that it
possessed a remarkable wistaria, and that 'Bishop Wilson, the
Metropolitan of India, was a student here'.

V

When John Hill at last took over as vice-principal in 1812, he was
only 25, and had already served a three years' apprenticeship under
Wilson. He was to hold office for almost forty years, being also
curate and then (from 1814) priest-in-charge of Hampton Gay,
then a thriving village (now only the church and ruined manor-
house remain) just north of Kidlington; he rode out there on his
horse (sustaining many a fall on the way) almost every Sunday to
conduct the services. From October 1820 until his death in 1855 he
kept a diary,[14] and we thus have a far more detailed picture of him
and his activities than of either of his predecessors. In its pages we
can see him interviewing admissions candidates, and presenting
undergraduates for matriculation and later for degrees; from time
to time doing business or settling the accounts with the principal;
attending convocation or lobbying (1834) old members to oppose
the proposed abolition of subscription to the Thirty-Nine Articles
at matriculation; greatly 'agitated' when students were found out
committing 'gross improprieties'; inaugurating (December 1838)
end-of-term collections—not the reading-out and discussion of
reports, as today, but oral examinations lasting twenty minutes on
texts he had lectured on. In November 1823 we observe him urging
the dying principal-elect (H. Wheatley) to repent of the excessive
'use of spirits' which has brought him to his present pass before he
faced his Judge—he was painfully aware that he faced the sack if
the patient resented his reproaches and recovered. Some of the
happiest entries are glimpses either of his affectionate family life or
of his Sunday visits to his 'dear flock' at Hampton Gay. All twenty
notebooks are crowded with devout exclamations and reflections.
    Like Crouch, Hill had early been a pupil of Edward Spencer. He

---

[14] It is at present kept in the Bodleian Library (MSS St Edmund Hall 66–67).

9. John Hill, vice-principal and earnest diarist

was a high calvinist himself, and under him the hall remained an important evangelical centre in Oxford, although as the years went by it was sending out fewer and fewer evangelicals of note. A junior contemporary[15] paints a kindly picture of the evening parties he gave for students, 'where prevailed tea and coffee, pietistic Low Church talk, prayers and hymnody of portentous length, yet palliated by the chance of sharing Bible or hymn-book with one of the host's four charming daughters'. But it seems that some of his charges were beginning to adopt a more extreme protestant stance. W. E. Gladstone, who was at Christ Church from 1828 to 1831, recalled[16] that 'a score or two of young men . . . nestled together in the small establishment of St Edmund Hall' who 'belonged to a school of ultra-Calvinism which lay far in advance of the ordinary evangelical tenets'. As an evangelical himself at that phase of his life, he knew what he was talking about; but the darker aspects of this religious extremism are underlined by yet a third contemporary, Thomas Mozley,[17] who as a tractarian wrote with a perhaps prejudiced pen. While speaking well of Hill as a scholar, and making the interesting point that a high proportion of hall men were from poor families who could not afford the expensive life of other colleges, he castigated its hothouse atmosphere, and the narrow vision and self-satisfied, introspective spirituality of many of its inmates, which tended to drive students with livelier intellectual interests to seek refuge in other societies.

Hill's time of office was clearly not the hall's most vigorous or glamorous period, but it was not exclusively given over to inward-looking religiosity. In the mid- and late thirties it had a flourishing debating society which gave prominence to the rule, 'No Theological subject shall form a question for Debate'. It met fortnightly in members' rooms, and the fixture-card covering 1835 to 1838 presents an appetizing range of subjects discussed. Some touched on themes of universal human import such as 'Happiness preponderates over misery in human life' and 'In old age the outliving of friends is a greater calamity than poverty'. Others raised issues of international politics, such as 'England ought not to interfere between Russia and Turkey' and 'Don Carlos has a constitutional

[15] W. Tuckwell, *Reminiscences of Oxford* (2nd edn., London, 1907), 96.
[16] *Gleanings of Past Years*, vii (London, 1879), 211–12.
[17] *Reminiscences, Chiefly of Oriel College and the Oxford Movement* (London, 1882), 241–6.

right to the throne of Spain'. Even the emancipation of women was timidly foreshadowed in a debate on 'The study of mathematics and the dead languages would form a suitable branch of female education'.

The hall also managed at this time, just occasionally, to produce an alumnus of brilliance, even of learned eccentricity. One such, in the former category, was William Fishburn Donkin,[18] who came from St Peter's School, York, matriculated in 1832, and rose to become Savilian professor of astronomy; he was equally a specialist in music, and wrote authoritatively (for his day) on both ancient Greek music and the theory of acoustics. Although he migrated to University College in 1834 on winning a classical scholarship, he kept up his links with the hall as mathematics lecturer for several years. His greatest friend there (they were known as Pylades and Orestes) was an eccentric genius, Solomon Caesar Malan[19] (1812– 94), who matriculated in 1833. Son of a protestant pastor at Geneva, against whom he rebelled, he was financed by his future father-in-law, who probably chose the hall because of its inexpensiveness. Young Malan, who was already well advanced in Hebrew, Sanskrit, and Arabic, but as yet spoke English poorly, begged to be allowed to write his examinations in French, German, Spanish, Italian, Latin, or Greek, but his petition was turned down. He nevertheless walked off with the Boden scholarship in Sanskrit, obtained a second in Greats (defective English was to blame), and later won the Pusey and Ellerton scholarship in Hebrew. While his public career embraced a spell as classics lecturer at Calcutta and then forty-one years as vicar of Broadwindsor, Dorset, his rare distinction was to be the outstanding orientalist of his day, with a command of seventy or eighty languages, including Chinese, Georgian, Turkish, and many Indian tongues. A superb calligrapher, a skilful draughtsman and water colourist, he presented the bulk of his vast, miscellaneous library (much of it of no Indological interest) to the newly founded Indian Institute in 1884. Many of his books were eventually dispersed throughout Bodley, but the core of the Malan collection was in recent years transferred with the rest of the library of the Institute to a room at the top of the New Bodleian. His portrait still hangs in the Indian Institute, in the offices of the librarian.

[18] See *DNB*.   [19] See *DNB*.

VI

Hill retired in 1851. He was worried by declining admissions, felt he was losing his touch and getting too old for the job (he was 63), and dreaded having to supervise study in new subjects (modern history and jurisprudence: 'in which I am totally ignorant') prescribed by recent examination statutes. He accepted the living of Wyke Regis, Dorset, where he died in 1855. As his successor, Principal Thompson nominated Edward Litton, also an evangelical, a fine scholar and a competent theologian, who had been a fellow of Oriel. In his diary for 17 November 1851 Hill noted: 'I bless God for his appointment' of 'a man at once so sound in doctrine, established in piety, and eminent in talent'.

Before he left the hall Hill had drafted the answers submitted on its behalf to the royal commission on the university set up in 1850 by Lord John Russell's first administration.[20] There was widespread resentment in Oxford at what was taken to be government interference, and even doubt as to its legality; several colleges, including Queen's, declined to collaborate with it. Principal Thompson shared these reservations, and in his first reply to the commissioners (12 November 1850) curtly remarked that he was unaware what information he could provide 'except such as relates to my office'. He evidently had second thoughts, but left it to Hill to assemble the information asked for. He dispatched this on 16 May 1851, expressing the hope in his covering letter that he would not be considered 'to imply any judgment as to the nature or expediency of the commission'.

Several interesting points emerge from his evidence. For example, while the hall did not exclude gentleman commoners, it discouraged them, and had accepted none for the past twenty-five years. Magdalen Hall, apparently, still took them, but they were on the way out in the colleges generally. Again, the hall had a bible clerk, nominated by the principal, who, as well as saying grace at dinner and reporting absentees from chapel, acted as library clerk and drafted testimonials for the principal and the vice-principal. For his pains he received between £40 and £45 p.a. as well as a reduction in battels. The vice-principal was sole tutor; 'necessity compels him . . . to attempt everything'. He gave lectures (i.e.

---

[20] For this and the next two paras. see Pp 1852, vol. 57, esp. pp. 383–6 of the Evidence appended (Hill's answers).

conducted classes) for 24–6 weeks in the year, the average number being 20–2 weekly. The subjects covered were, on the one hand, the Greek Testament, the Old Testament, and the Thirty-Nine Articles, on the other hand Latin and English composition, two Greek and one or two Latin authors, a treatise of Aristotle, and either logic or Euclid and algebra; there was no class in higher mathematics. Three or four undergraduates were reading with private tutors; these were presumably men working for honours. Chapel attendance was strictly enforced each day on pain of 'a literary exercise', and on Mondays (a feature unique to the hall) each junior member was required to hand the vice-principal a written summary 'of one, at least, of the discourses he had heard on the preceding day'. The hall had accommodation for twenty-seven undergraduates (it actually had twenty-three on its books in 1851). The gate was shut nightly at 10 p.m.; admittance after that was reported to the principal (presumably because the vice-principal lived out), and a graduated fine had to be paid to the porter.

The commissioners were much concerned about the high cost of an Oxford education, and pressed searching inquiries under this head. Hill was able to report that a man's average battels in 1849 came to £32 for the year; including room-rent, tuition, university dues, and other charges his total bill amounted to £68. 'One or two of the members who have recently graduated here have not exceeded £240 in the amount of their colleges bills during their four years of residence', including everything except clothing and travel expenses. University College reported that the average bill covering all items had been £103. 9s. 0d. in 1849, while Wadham's spokesman stated that the lowest amount he had known an undergraduate to live on in his society was 'somewhat under £150 p.a.'. At Magdalen Hall the figure for battels alone for 1849 varied from £91. 9s. 2d. at the highest to £55. 19s. 1d. at the lowest. It is not surprising that the commissioners professed themselves well satisfied with our hall. As they remarked,[21] 'In the Halls which are unendowed large payments may be with some reason exacted from the Students, and yet it appears from the Evidence that St Edmund Hall is at present one of the cheapest places of education in Oxford.'

---

[21] Pp 1852, vol. 57, Report, 32.

VII

The hall's long identification with evangelical Anglicanism came to an abrupt end with the death of Principal W. Thompson in September 1854. Both his immediate successors were, as it happened (it was no high-church plot on the part of Queen's), adherents of the tractarian, or catholic, movement in the church of England, and understandably nominated vice-principals whom they expected to be likewise sympathetic to it. Even so, although the hall under them began to acquire, and was to retain for more than a century, a leaning towards high Anglicanism, they did not make it a distinctively tractarian centre. John Barrow DD (1854–61), was a die-hard who, as a fellow of Queen's, had recently addressed an open letter[22] to Gladstone protesting against the commissioners' proposals that fellowships and scholarships at the college should be opened to a wider world than Cumberland and Westmorland; as a compromise alternative he had suggested that the college should take over the hall and use it as an 'open' annexe. Though junior to them, he was a friend of leading tractarians; these included J. H. Newman, who, while disclaiming that they had been intimates, was later to report[23] that 'he used to make use of me as a sort of confessor'. The second, John Branthwaite, MA (1861–6), also a fellow of Queen's, had been headmaster of Lancing College, Sussex, a school recently founded to promote the ideals of the Oxford movement. His principalship, inaugurated on 30 April 1861, was cut short when he was drowned in July 1864 when bathing by himself in Morecambe Bay. Lancing old boys recalled[24] him as a precise and scrupulous scholar, not very practical, but generous, who was at ease with people of most types, was nicknamed 'Brandy Snaps', but never, in spite of heroic efforts, mastered the art of swimming.

If Branthwaite's principalship was uneventful except for its tragic close, Barrow's opened with controversy and ended in personal disaster. Within weeks of his admission he found himself faced with what threatened to become a major constitutional row.[25] A group

---

[22] See J. R. Magrath, *The Queen's College*, ii. 163–5.
[23] C. S. Dessain and T. Gornall (edd.), *The Letters and Diaries of J. H. Newman* (London and Oxford, 1961–84), xxix. 231.
[24] See B. W. T. Handford, *Lancing 1848–1930* (Oxford, 1933), 65–94.
[25] J. R. Magrath, *The Queen's College*, ii. 165 (he confuses the petitioner, G. Hill, with the former vice-principal, J. Hill).

of thirty-six aularians, doctors and masters, submitted a petition to the university commissioners calling in question the claim of Queen's to nominate the principal; the appointment should be handed back to the hall's masters of arts, with whom (they alleged) it had rested in medieval times, and its 'proper independence' thereby restored. In January 1855 the leader of the malcontents, the Revd George Hill, made public a letter he had addressed to Barrow himself, in which he developed these points at greater length and proposed that the electoral body should be 'a standing Board, to consist, perhaps, of seven graduated members on the books of the Hall'. Fortunately for Barrow, the petitioners' target was not himself but Queen's, which was fully capable of standing up for its rights. In April 1855 its masterful young bursar, William Thomson (shortly to become provost, and later the college's third archbishop of York), published a crushing rejoinder, exposing the petition's lack of historical and legal basis. Understandably, the commissioners took no action; but the episode provides evidence of the persistence, and growth, of the dissatisfaction with the college's one-sided control of which we detected signs at Principal W. Thompson's installation.[26]

It was six years later, on 28 February 1861, that disaster struck.[27] That morning W. Hill, a graduate student, accompanied by three undergraduates, went to the vice-principal, H. P. Liddon, 'with a most painful report about the dear Pr.'. It is clear that it charged him with sexual misconduct with J. T. Browne, a second-year commoner; either then or later Browne produced a written 'deposition'. Next day Hill called on the principal in the morning, Liddon (who had sent a note in the afternoon) at 7 p.m. This latter visit resulted in 'a most painful scene'; Barrow admitted the charges, showing great 'self-reproach and humility'. There followed agonizing weeks, with Dr Pusey, Mr Keble, and other trusted friends being privately consulted. First Liddon, and then Pusey, walked out to Shotover with Barrow and held heart-to-heart talks with him. There was general agreement that he must resign, ostensibly on the grounds of health, and on 26 March he left Oxford, retreating (like other Victorian men similarly trapped) to

---

[26] See above p. 67.
[27] This para., with quotations in it, is drawn from Liddon's diary (kept at Liddon House, London W1) for Jan.–Apr. 1861. Liddon nowhere spells out Barrow's offence, but there can be no doubt of its nature.

France. On 9 April his 'Deed of Resignation', signed in Boulogne, was brought by hand to Liddon, who on 12 April broke the news to the provost of Queen's (W. Thomson). The provost was 'v. kind and courteous', assumed temporary financial responsibility for the hall, drafted a notice for *The Times*, and remarked that Barrow must be deranged—in fact, he had long thought he was. Later he begged that Browne's incriminating deposition might 'be destroyed by fire'. On 13 April Liddon waited on the vice-chancellor and told him that the principal had resigned 'thro' mental derangement'. The day before, Barrow had written[28] to him privately explaining that he was giving ill health, 'pecuniary considerations', but 'not Romanism' as causes of his retirement; only to his most intimate friends was he mentioning 'other things which I could not well write about . . .'.

What happened to Browne is not known. There was talk of expelling him, but this was dropped. His family promised to 'keep quiet for some time'. He himself was sent away for a while with his sister, duly furnished by Liddon with 'a scheme of occupation' and the assurance of his prayers; but he never returned to the hall. For Barrow himself the sad little episode was to have a positive outcome. After living as a recluse in France, he was received into the Roman Catholic church in 1864, changed his name to William Bernard, and in 1866 went out to the Jesuit mission at Madura, in India, where he eventually became headmaster. In 1873 he returned to France for reasons of health, was ordained a Roman Catholic priest in 1876, and died at the Apostolic School at Bordeaux on 1 January 1880. By now his reputation stood so high that its rector wanted to publish a memoir of him, and wrote to Newman, now a prince of the church, seeking information about his university days. At once Barrow's old friends, Anglican and Roman Catholic, closed ranks, and after consulting them the cardinal agreed that the less said about his Oxford career the better.[29] The story which gained currency as a result of their cover-up was that Barrow had been forced into resignation through making a mess of his own and the hall's finances. His supposed Roman leanings were also dragged in, although they do not seem to have been especially remarked on at

---

[28] This letter is in a file of Barrow's correspondence with Liddon kept at Keble College.
[29] See *Letters and Diaries of J. H. Newman*, xxix. 233 (letter to Fr. A. Batut, SJ, with the misleading footnote 4).

the time, and he himself explicitly denied that they had influenced him.

VIII

Although the total of undergraduates in residence dropped slightly in the two years following Barrow's resignation, both his and Branthwaite's principalships saw a welcome restoration both of numbers and of academic repute. The annual intake now averaged seven; among those admitted were two later celebrities—John Stainer, organist, composer, and pioneer of musicology; and Peter Oronhyatekha, chief of the Mohawk Indians, who had impressed the Prince of Wales so much during his visit to Canada in 1860 that he placed him under the care of his personal physician, Professor Sir Henry Acland, regius professor of medicine, and arranged for him to come to Oxford. Oronhyatekha did not matriculate, and his stay at the hall was brief; but he was to become revered as a medical practitioner among his own people as well as first Supreme Ranger of the Independent Order of Foresters.[30] For three or four of these years (1859–62) the hall had a couple of lecturers on its roll, one in mathematics and natural science, the other in modern history (the latter was Montagu Burrows, commander RN, from 1862 Chichele professor). Their function was to cope with the newer honours subjects, the prospect of which John Hill had found so daunting in 1850; the routine grind of the pass teaching still required by the great majority of the students, as well as the general supervision of the hall, continued to rest with the vice-principals.

There were three of these in this period. Barrow's first was the Revd Henry Walford, who had been at school at Rugby under Arnold and liked to encourage the belief that he was the 'Slogger' in Tom Hughes's *Tom Brown's Schooldays* (1857). Although more of a muscular Christian than a strict tractarian, he subsequently became headmaster of Lancing.[31] He was succeeded in 1859 by Liddon; and when Liddon moved back to his old college, Christ Church, in 1862, the Revd Charles Eddy, a fellow of Queen's, took

[30] For a brief account of Oronhyatekha, and of the presentation of his (posthumous) portrait to the college, see *SEHM* (1968–9), 14–15. A room in the college named after him contains relics of his stay, including his tomahawk.
[31] See B. W. T. Handford, *Lancing 1848–1930*, 95–7.

10. H. P. Liddon, from the cartoon by Spy (Sir Leslie Ward, 1851–1922)

his place. The fact that the vice-principal could be married was always an inducement.

Of the three much the most noteworthy was Henry Parry Liddon.[32] A devoted tractarian, disciple and friend of Keble and Pusey, he had been the first vice-principal of Cuddesdon theological college, recently founded in the grounds of the bishop of Oxford's palace, but had been forced to leave as a result of evangelical attacks. He found a congenial refuge at the hall in 1859, and seems to have had a great regard and affection for Barrow, to whom he dutifully submitted his sermons before delivery. Like his evangelical predecessors, he was chiefly interested in the spiritual welfare of those under his charge, and started expositions of the Greek testament, first in his own rooms, and then as numbers grew in the dining-hall; later he had to hold them in the halls of Queen's and of Christ Church. As pro-proctor he was more troubled about the interior state of any young man he had to arrest than about his petty misdemeanour, and a typical entry in his diary records, 'A long talk with our Hall messenger boy about his soul. He is sadly ignorant of Divine truth.' On a practical level he took in hand the restoration of the chapel, calling on the fashionable architect, G. E. Street, for advice. Street, he noted, 'wishes to Gothicize' it, and so it was perhaps fortunate that the new principal, Branthwaite, vetoed his plan. He had greater success in getting a small organ (the first the hall had possessed) installed; it was placed at the south-east corner of the ~~sanctuary~~ chancel.

A delayed but more lasting fruit of his refurbishment plans was the remodelling, in 1865, of the tracery of the east window (originally eight arched panels, arranged in two tiers of four surmounted by a large circular light supported by two tiny ones), and the insertion in it of the present stained glass, designed in the main by Edward Burne-Jones (the panels depicting the men of Galilee and the three Maries at the Sepulchre were by William Morris) and executed by Morris's manufacturing and decorating firm.

Liddon coped courageously with the crisis of Barrow's exposure, which shook his sensitive nature to its depths. A serious attack of illness in 1862 obliged him to resign from his position at the hall, but he was already becoming widely known for his sermons in the chapel (the manuscripts of several of these survive), in the

---

[32] On Liddon at the hall see *Henry Parry Liddon, 1829–1929: A Centenary Memoir* (London, 1929), 29–33.

university, and in the world outside. It was at the hall in fact that he laid the foundations of his dazzling career as a pulpit orator, to reach its climax when he was canon of St Paul's, which years later would lead the *Oxford Magazine* to describe him,[33] a few months before his death, as 'the most finished preacher of our day . . . the Bossuet of the nineteenth century'.

[33] *OM* 21 (1890), 341.

VIII

Take-over Threats Averted

I

THE half-century from Principal Branthwaite's untimely drowning
to the outbreak of World War I was almost the most critical in the
hall's history. Twice it came closer to extinction than at any time
except the mid-sixteenth century. This might at first sight appear
surprising, for it was in a healthy state throughout, respected in
Oxford and constructively diversifying its internal life. But this was
an age of reform, with the university and its institutions being
dragged into the modern world; when so much was changing, the
hall was vulnerable to the impatience of reformers as well as to the
ambitions of the powerful. Its success in surmounting the crisis was
due to the tenacity, and also the prestige, of a principal who held on
for forty-nine years, refusing to budge until its future seemed
secure.

Edward Moore,[1] DD, installed in October 1864, was a graduate
of Pembroke with first classes in mathematics and classics in both
moderations and finals. Son of a Cardiff physician, he was one of
the first 'open' fellows of Queen's, i.e. fellows chosen from outside
the two counties, Cumberland and Westmorland, favoured by its
founder. His long reign was an exceptionally busy one, for as well
as being head of house, full-time tutor, and (admittedly largely
absentee) rector of Gatcombe, he was active in university affairs,
serving on hebdomadal council (for twenty years), as curator of the
Sheldonian Theatre and the Taylor Institution, once as senior
proctor, and on a variety of boards. But while admired in Oxford as
a teacher (especially of Aristotle's *Ethics* and *Poetics*), it was as a
Dante scholar that he attained European renown. In 1863, in
preparation for a holiday in Italy, he had picked up some Italian
from the Taylorian lecturer, Vital De Tivoli, a passionate lover of
Dante. Henceforth Dante became his absorbing study too, and he
made particularly important contributions to the textual criticism

---

[1] See *DNB* suppl. vol. (1912–21) and *Proceedings of the British Academy*, 7
(1915–16), 575–84.

87

11. Edward Moore, DD, FBA. From his portrait at the Hall

of both the *Divina Commedia* and the *Convivio*. It was natural that he should be the founder (1870), and throughout his life the guiding spirit, of the Oxford Dante Society, and that he should hold special lectureships on Dante at both London and Oxford. Honours were heaped upon him, including in 1901 corresponding membership of the Accademia della Crusca and in 1906 a fellowship of the recently founded (1902) British Academy. As recently as 1969, more than fifty years after his death, a fresh printing of his four-volume *Studies in Dante* was called for.

Moore was only 29 when appointed. For his first few years he performed the functions of vice-principal himself, employing chaplain-lecturers to help him out with services and teaching. The first (1864–9), Thomas Kelly Cheyne, was to become a brilliant if eccentric Old Testament scholar, the second (1869–71), Andrew Wallace Milroy, a respected professor of Latin at London. In 1871 he reverted to traditional practice, and from then until 1913 had a succession of five vice-principals, almost all men of above-average ability. One, for example, Ernest Nathaniel Bennett (1893–5), had a colourful career as soldier, war correspondent, and member of Parliament (he was the first layman to be vice-principal). Another, H. G. Wild (1895–1903), was a future bishop of Newcastle. A third, S. L. Ollard (1903–13), was a scholarly historian of the Oxford movement.

For most of this period Moore and his vice-principals had no tutorial assistants. There was no need for lecturers of the kind briefly experimented with in 1859–62, for from 1865 Queen's and the hall had an arrangement under which members of either society were free to attend all lectures given by the other; the advantage was by no means wholly in the hall's favour, for Moore's own lectures were eagerly attended. In 1895, however, probably because of the large number of men reading the subject, the hall began retaining a lecturer in theology. Like his predecessors, Moore himself handled the hall accounts and all bursarial matters, although Ollard had to shoulder the day-to-day burden in his last decade. Printing was one of his hobbies, and he delighted to send out battels accounts, hall prospectuses, and other notices which he himself had printed on his private press in the lodgings.

II

Moore's appointment coincided with a lively debate on 'university extension', i.e. on how an Oxford education could be extended, as progressive Victorian opinion demanded, to wider, less-affluent sections of society. The new private halls, inaugurated in 1855, had hardly touched the problem and fresh possibilities were now being canvassed, including the foundation of a large new college or hall to be run on economical lines. The five older halls were quick to perceive the threat such proposals held to themselves, but also ways in which the new mood could be exploited to their own advantage. Dr D. P. Chase, principal of St Mary Hall, rushed out a pamphlet in 1865 claiming that his hall and St Alban Hall were already providing, by the ingenious device of all-inclusive charges, the cut-price university education called for. Not to be outdone, Moore argued, in *Frugal Education Attainable Under the Existing Collegiate System* (1867), that at his hall the full student life could be lived even more cheaply than at the other halls without sacrificing the traditional system of battels and other charges, which had the immense advantage of teaching young men to manage their own affairs and discover the value of money ('generally, I imagine, a disappointing discovery'). He added that St Edmund Hall had ample space available nearby (e.g. to the south of the quadrangle) which, judiciously developed, could more than double its accommodation. It would be much more sensible for the university to expand resources already at its disposal than to embark on a costly new foundation.

The university did not itself create a new college or hall, but neither did it take up Moore's (and Chase's) suggestion that the existing halls were tailor-made for keen students of modest means. Instead, it enacted two measures which filled him with apprehension. First, it removed (1870) the age-old requirement that under-graduates must reside for virtually their entire course in their colleges, and permitted residence in lodgings. Secondly, it inaugurated in 1868 the 'unattached students system', making it possible for men to become members of the university under the supervision of a delegacy without belonging to a college or a hall. In his response (1873)[2] to the commission of 1872 inquiring into the

---

[2] Pp 1873, vol. 37, Report, Part. II, 885

property and income of Oxford and Cambridge Moore argued that these innovations spelled disaster for the halls, which were likely to be deprived of the two classes on which they depended for their intake—(1) men desirous of living 'as quietly and economically as possible', and (2) men whom colleges could not admit at short notice owing to the pressure on their accommodation.

Moore's evidence to the commissioners is especially illuminating for the picture it presents, within the limits of the questions asked, of material conditions at the hall in the 1870s.[3] Its total income for 1872, he reported, from external sources (quitrent, investments) was £13. 5s. 0d., from internal sources (room-rents, fees, and other charges) £1037. 14s. 4d.; in addition it received just over £400 net (after deducting rates, taxes, and curate's stipend) from Gatcombe. The principal's emoluments, inclusive of his Gatcombe stipend, amounted to £1048. 10s. 1d.; but out of this he had to defray the vice-principal's stipend (for this no figure was stated). In that year £10. 3s. 0d. was expended on scholars and exhibitioners (exclusive of remissions of room-rents, tuition, and other charges), £263. 19s. 10d. on servants' wages, £22. 11s. 6d. on the library, and £205. 15s. 8d. on buildings and repairs. This last sum was provided out of an annual charge imposed on all junior members. The buildings were declared to be in a satisfactory state of repair, and to be properly insured. No audit, Moore had to confess, was made of the hall accounts.

III

The hall, with the other three halls (the fifth, Magdalen Hall, had been incorporated as Hertford College in 1874), naturally came under the scrutiny of the 1877 statutory commission on Oxford, which was specifically empowered to close down or amalgamate societies where this was considered desirable. Evidence was submitted by D. P. Chase, representing his own hall, St Alban Hall, and New Inn Hall, and by Moore. Chase made it clear[4] that the plight of the other three halls was precarious. Desperately poor, with two of them relying on the throw-outs of colleges, their position had been undermined by the 'unattached students system'; the proper course for St Mary Hall and St Alban Hall would be to

---

[3] Ibid., Report, Part I, 129; Part II, 885.
[4] Pp 1881, vol. 56, *Minutes of Evidence*, 36–41.

merge with Oriel and Merton respectively. By contrast St Edmund Hall, he predicted, had a useful future. It had not only an endowment (Gatcombe), although an unsatisfactory one since the parishioners were unhappy about their rector's non-residence, but 'a working arrangement with Queen's which enables it to give as good tuition as any Queen's man can have'.

Moore too painted[5] a bright picture of his hall. It had never, in his or his predecessors' times, stooped to accepting undergraduates 'obliged to leave other colleges through their own fault'; and so far from students deserting it to become 'unattached', the traffic had recently been in the reverse direction. It was well placed, he urged, to provide a full university education without any sacrifice of social or collegiate life at a very low cost; and he submitted figures showing that a man's annual expenses, clothes and travelling excluded, need not exceed £100 or even £90 a year. Its accommodation was small, twenty-eight rooms, but this could be enlarged by taking over nearby properties. His main plea was that, if the halls—his own hall in particular—were to survive, they needed adequate endowment. He added that, if funds were to be diverted by a college for the support of poor students at a hall, it was fair that that college should have a voice in their selection and in the application of the funds. If this resulted in the emergence of some kind of governing body for the hall, this should be welcomed as giving it a more public character and greater stability. If a hall were to receive endowment, the principal could not expect to remain 'as autocratic and irresponsible' as he now was—a position which in his opinion was in any case 'an undesirable anomaly'.

It was a third witness, J. R. Magrath, the able and masterful pro-provost (soon to be provost) of Queen's, whose proposals[6] for the hall carried the day. Claiming that the non-collegiate system was not working satisfactorily, he argued that the most constructive way of meeting the needs of 'poor and deserving students' would be to place the existing halls under the wings of colleges. As regards our hall, its administration should be taken over by Queen's, which should maintain it as a related but separate community of poor students, subsidizing their living costs and tuition. It was a scheme along these lines that the commissioners adopted. While ordering the other three halls to be completely merged with colleges, they

---

[5] Pp 1881, vol. 56, *Minutes of Evidence*, 41–3.
[6] Ibid., *Minutes of Evidence*, 142–4.

treated St Edmund Hall as a separate case, permitting its continued existence but no longer as an independent institution. Instead, they decreed[7] that, when the principalship fell vacant or its present holder agreed to submit to their statute, a 'partial union' should be effected between it and Queen's under which it would become a poor students' annexe of the college. While its chapel, library, and dining-hall would be kept separate, its buildings, revenues, and internal life would be under the control of Queen's. The principal, who would be a fellow of the college, would function as the hall's dean and tutor, admitting students subject to regulations laid down by the governing body. Queen's would pay his salary, would be responsible for repairs and maintenance, and would provide twenty-four exhibitions of not less than £25 a year for each of the hall's student inmates. An important ingredient of the scheme was that these should live segregated from Queen's men, since only so (as Magrath had hinted[8] in his evidence) could the stricter and more economical regime aimed at be observed.

IV

The commissioners' scheme was a bitter disappointment for Moore. He must have been relieved that the hall had escaped from suppression, an option they had considered, but while he had wanted it, in return for some endowment, to make its contribution to solving the 'poor students' problem, he had never envisaged it passing so completely under the control of Queen's, still less its being reduced to an exclusively eleemosynary dependency. His incautious words about being ready to accept some diminution of its autonomy had been taken farther than he had intended. As it was, there was nothing he could do but soldier on in the hope that the unpalatable plan might be somehow frustrated or else lapse.

As events worked out, the hall prospered under his leadership, and in 1903 was complimented[9] on being 'one of the most patriotic as well as best conducted bodies in the University'. Although fluctuating unpredictably, matriculations averaged about ten a year throughout most of his reign; in his last decade they were sharply

---

[7] See *Statutes Made by the Commissioners under the Universities Act 1877* (the statute was approved by the Queen in Council on 3 May 1882).

[8] Pp 1881, vol. 56, *Minutes of Evidence*, 142.

[9] OM (25 Feb. 1903).

increasing, with, for example, eighteen freshmen in 1909. Although total admissions to the university were rising steadily, this must be reckoned a creditable achievement when one bears in mind the pulling-power after 1870 of Keble, a highly successful new foundation which drew on much the same clientele and aimed at a similarly economical life-style. Numbers actually in residence hovered around twenty-five to twenty-seven until the end of the century, and then began to increase, and in 1907 reached thirty-eight, in 1912 forty-eight. The social background of hall entrants was much less affluent than that of Oxford entrants generally, with less than half in the late 1890s, compared with three-fourths in the university at large, coming from public schools of whatever grade; even so, one or even two a year came from top schools. The gap was gradually narrowing, however, and in 1911–14 the percentages of public school matriculands for the hall and the university were respectively 62.5 per cent and 65.4 per cent (although the majority of the hall's intake came from lesser public schools).[10]

Moore recorded the men admitted each year, along with details of their subsequent academic performance, in his register, a stout volume (actually, two volumes bound together in one) which he kept methodically from 1867 to 1913, assigning a separate page to each. While this confirms that he did not accept rejects, it also shows that, in his earlier years at any rate, a few tended to migrate to other colleges, usually on obtaining an award, while throughout a sizeable proportion of those admitted fell by the way through being 'plucked' in their examinations. Independent statistics indicate that of those matriculating in the sample year 1893/4 more than half never proceeded to the BA; for 1898/9 the proportion had dropped to a quarter. These figures should not shock, for the failure rate was, by modern standards, surprisingly high in the university as a whole. Where the hall stood out was in having, for most of Moore's reign, a higher proportion of passmen than the colleges. By the early 1900s this disparity was being corrected, and in 1907, 1908, and 1913 the numbers gaining honours (history, English literature, Oriental languages, and mathematics were represented as well as theology) were respectively eight, nine, and fifteen; in the last year more than half the men in residence were reading for

---

[10] I owe these, and other figures in this section, to Mark Curthoys.

honours. Another development in Moore's time was the gradual decline in the proportion of hall graduates entering the ministry. In sample years before 1850 it had been as high as 67 per cent, as against 49.5 per cent for the whole university; but in the two sample years 1878/9 and 1897/8 it dropped to 37.5 per cent, as against 23.5 per cent for Oxford generally. There was a parallel increase in the proportion entering the teaching profession. Few, if any, are recorded as entering the army, the government service, or commerce.

V

It was in Moore's time that the corporate life of the hall, with the range of student activities characteristic of modern Oxford, began to take shape. A junior common room was established, apparently in the early 1890s; the boat club, soon followed by other societies, is recorded as holding its meetings there from March 1894. It originally occupied the ground-floor room of the cottage south of the chapel. The debating society was unremittingly active throughout the whole period; there were usually bumper attendances, with liquid refreshment and specified brands of pipe-tobacco provided. Ladies were occasionally invited as guests, and in 1902 a debate was held with ladies participating. Theological issues were excluded from discussion; to deal with them a Guild of St Edmund, with an office to be recited before each meeting, was founded in 1887. In 1909 the Essay Society came into existence, with S. L. Ollard, the vice-principal, as the first president.

Despite shortage of manpower, the hall participated enthusiastically in the cult of athleticism and organized games which began gripping the universities in the 1850s and 1860s. The boat club, founded in 1861, was an all-absorbing focus of interest; its surviving minute-books and log-books vividly recapture its endless training outings, and its ambitious plans, occasional successes, and all too frequent disillusionments. For years it rented a barge between Folly Bridge and Salter's yard, and it first succeeded in entering a boat for Eights week, at the bottom of the river, in 1874. Immense pressure was put on freshmen to take up rowing; when one youth in 1902 had the temerity to declare that he preferred football, and in any case could not in conscience devote more than three hours a week to sport, the vice-principal acidly observed that

95

any gentleman with such sentiments 'might do well to become Unattached'. As a matter of fact, football, both association and rugby, and cricket flourished side by side with, though as somewhat poor relations of, rowing; as numbers were so small, oarsmen frequently had to abandon the river for the playing-field. For example, the log-book for February 1887 contains the entries 'No boating owing to Rugby Union Match with Wadham', and (a week later) 'No boating owing to Socker match with Unattached'. Moore himself once commented[11] on the boat club that 'it promoted corporate feeling, involved a good deal of self-discipline, and was a very healthy influence—although it sometimes interfered a little with the work for the Schools.'

<h1 style="text-align:center">VI</h1>

Lively impressions of undergraduate life under Moore can be gleaned from a diary which Charles H. Fullmer, who matriculated in April 1885, kept for his two final years. He overlapped with his elder brother Christopher, who had transferred from 'the unattached' on being appointed organ scholar at the hall. In his jottings we can see Charles calling periodically on 'the Chief' to settle his battels or get certificates signed, attending his lectures on the *Ethics* (on one occasion, he recalls with glee, Moore rebuked the Queen's men present for cribbing), or being reminded by him by letter that term had already begun and it was time he was back. Quite early he formed a Sunday breakfast-party with four others; after breakfasting in the rooms of one of them, they would troop off to St Barnabas for 'the High Service'. He was punctilious in calling on freshmen—and in noting whether they returned his calls. Lunches or teas in his own or a friend's rooms, always with heart-to-heart discussions, were constant features of his life, and in Eights week he clubbed with a fellow-student to entertain the eight to breakfast. He rarely missed the debating society, and occasionally turned up at union debates, but it was games, especially cricket and 'boating', that fascinated him most. His pages abound in graphic accounts of outings in pairs or fours, and we have a poignant description of the hall's ill luck in Eights week 1887, in spite of its boat being cheered on 'by most of the colleges'. Next year the eight

---

[11] *Oxford Review* (23 May 1903) (in a speech at a dinner in his honour).

My College Rooms.
(Looking from the window)

Drawn October. 29. 1887

(Looking towards the window)

Drawn October. 31. 1887

12. Charles Fullmer's sitting-room at the top of Staircase 4 (the twin-light window was replaced by four lights in 1932)

had to be taken off the river because 'the Chief' forbade two oarsmen suffering from mumps to row; he narrowly escaped a motion of censure because of his 'interference'.

Trinity term 1887 was particularly rich in excitements. On 25 May the eight was hosted to a wine which lasted till 1 a.m.; 'the Vice', who had contributed a dozen of champagne, had to ring his hand-bell at midnight to quieten the revellers. Next week there was a smoking concert in the dining-hall, with music and 'very good comic songs'; while on 15 June his friend Tucker won a bet of 6d. by running naked across the quadrangle between 10 and 11 p.m. Later in the year Charles and his friends put pressure on 'the Chief' to sanction an early celebration of communion on St Edmund's day (was this the first such pious commemoration?), and a few days later 'the Vice' entertained all the students to a wine at which everyone (including St Edmund) was ceremonially toasted in order of precedence. Interspersed with social and sporting activities are notes of lectures attended, papers sat, and vivas taken as Charles progressed in easygoing style through the pass school. He sat his last 'group' (in divinity) in December 1887, and was successful in his viva. He was thus able to skip the Lent term, and to return late for his final term, having no specific academic tasks. On 13 June 1888 he called on 'the Chief' at 9 p.m., paid outstanding fees, and got him to sign a certificate of residence; next day he graduated BA, breakfasting with 'the Vice' and being presented by him because Moore was otherwise engaged. His mother, for whom he had booked a room at the Great Western Hotel and whom he later took on a tour of the colleges, proudly witnessed the ceremony.

VII

Early in 1903 the storm-clouds which had built up menacingly in 1877–81 suddenly burst over the hall. In January the crown, in recognition of his literary distinction, nominated Moore to a residentiary canonry at Canterbury, and he accepted it. His initial intention, of which he made no secret, was to resign as principal, for the two offices were not normally held in conjunction. No one knew better than he that the 1877 commissioners' statute was scheduled to come into operation immediately he retired, but he seems to have hoped that opinion in the university would enforce either the amendment of its most objectionable features, or better still, its abrogation. What he could not anticipate, and was kept in the dark about until the last moment, was the reaction of Queen's to his appointment. Although the statute had been passed at its instigation, the college led by Provost Magrath now decided that it was unworkable, and further that the only practicable alternative to the 'partial union' it proposed was total take-over. Without giving notice to Moore, the governing body rushed through, by a bare majority, a statute providing for the 'complete union' of the hall and the college; the principalship would be suppressed, and members of the hall would be entitled to membership of Queen's. The approval of council having been obtained, it was arranged that this statute[12] should be brought before congregation on 24 February.

Moore first set eyes on the statute when he opened his *University Gazette* on Tuesday 17 February. On 23 February he circulated members of congregation with a flysheet (printed on his own press) protesting against the 'entirely wanton and gratuitous' destruction of the hall proposed, and next day no fewer than 151 members assembled in convocation house. The debate was one charged with emotion, for the principal antagonists, Moore and Magrath, were lifelong friends; Moore, too, was painfully aware that he was attacking a dearly loved college which had recently elected him an honorary fellow. He pleaded with the university not to sanction the suppression of a flourishing and useful society which was also one of its most ancient foundations; and he rammed this latter point home by observing that had Dante (1265–1321) ever visited Oxford, he would have seen St Edmund Hall at work, while across the lane there were still only green fields.[13] The matter was clinched when the university registrar, T. H. Grose, himself a fellow of Queen's, disclosed with some embarrassment that the college had failed to carry the amending statute in proper form since it required a two-thirds majority; this had not been obtained, and he doubted whether it could have been. The preamble to the statute was decisively rejected by 94 votes to 57.

The rejection was a personal triumph for Moore, and delighted the *Oxford Magazine*. 'Oxford opinion', it remarked,[14] 'has now come round to the view that the extinction of small Societies is not

---

[12] For the text, along with that of the commissioners' statute it purported to amend, see *OUG* 33 (1902–3), 338–40.

[13] See *The Times* (5 Sept. 1906), 6.   [14] (25 Feb. 1903).

in itself desirable . . . To destroy the hall at this moment would be an offence not only against sentiment, but also against prudence.' On paper the commissioners' statute was now due to come into effect, but Moore, heartened by the vote, was beginning to form the idea of preventing this. His resolve was strengthened when he was entertained to what was intended as a farewell dinner by over 100 old members in the town hall on 28 May 1903. At this gathering— the first aularian reunion ever to be held—the prospects and position of the hall were discussed, and there was unanimous agreement that no effort should be spared to secure its future. Moore therefore cancelled his plans for resignation, and with the sanction[15] of the prime minister retained the principalship along with the canonry. There ensued a protracted stalemate, for Queen's was not yet in a mood for compromise. Moore settled in Canterbury in the long vacation of 1903; he let out the lodgings (for several years they were occupied by A. J. Carlyle, the historian of medieval political thought, and his family), but came up to the hall for a short stay at the beginning of each term, living in a student's set, to collect fees and transact business with under-graduates. For the next ten years the day-to-day administration of the hall was in the capable, if often overburdened, hands of the vice-principal, S. L. Ollard, who from the moment of his appointment identified himself completely with its interests.

VIII

In spite of a largely absentee principal and the problematical future facing it, this was an exhilarating period in the hall's history. Numbers and academic achievements were on the upturn; its corporate spirit was the envy of other colleges. Among junior members destined for prominence were J. W. C. Wand, later to become archbishop of Brisbane and then bishop of London, and Percy Alfred Scholes (B. Mus. 1908), a musicologist internationally renowned. But the real drama of the decade was the persistent campaign waged by Moore and Ollard, with eager aularian back-ing, to bring about the replacement of the hated commissioners' statute. Their dream was at least to preserve the hall's present independent status, better still to bring it under the oversight of a

<hr />

[15] So *DNB*, suppl. vol. (1912–21) (the PM was A. J. Balfour).

university delegacy or (as Keble at the time) of a council of governors. A turning-point was a dinner held in London, with Moore in the chair, on 8 October 1908, at which a strong committee of past and present members was appointed both to promote the cause and also to raise an endowment fund, indispensable (in Moore's view) if independence were to be obtained. In May 1909, just before its great annual meeting, Moore addressed a reasoned petition to Queen's asking it to agree to the rescission of the commissioners' statute; along with the petition he sent a memorial signed by 183 resident members of congregation (including virtually all heads of houses), calling for the preservation of the hall as an independent society. The college maintained silence until November, when it rejected the petition.

In the deadlock Moore took the inspired step of personally approaching the new, vigorous chancellor, Lord Curzon of Kedleston, in his capacity as visitor, and submitted to him provisions for a revised constitution. Curzon, who was then actively engaged in university reform, responded sympathetically. His intervention proved decisive. At a meeting over which he presided in person, hebdomadal council resolved to take the matter up and discuss with Queen's the adoption of a scheme along the lines Moore had suggested. There followed months of delays, but by June 1911 the opposition in Queen's, after a dramatic internal upheaval, had collapsed, and the college indicated its readiness to co-operate constructively with the proposed changes. In Michaelmas term 1911 council drafted the necessary statute and in Trinity term 1912, after legal difficulties had been overcome, it was accepted by congregation without opposition. It was approved by the king in council in February 1913.

This statute,[16] the first written constitution of its own the hall had ever received, sufficiently met the aspirations of Moore and his allies. It preserved, of course, the ancient right of Queen's to appoint the principal, as also its possession of the freehold of the site and buildings; indeed, it empowered the college to take forceful action if the principal should prove negligent in the maintenance and insurance of the latter. But in its preamble it specifically decreed that the hall should continue 'as a place of education, religion, and learning separate from' Queen's. Further, it brought

---

[16] For the text see *Statuta et Decreta Universitatis Oxoniensis* (1913), 557–602.

the hall in some degree under the aegis of the university, requiring the principal to present an annual report to congregation, to have the hall's accounts audited by the university auditors and published with the university and colleges accounts, and to be himself subject like professors to the visitatorial board. As in the past, the principal remained personally responsible for the upkeep and insurance of the buildings, receiving all room-rents, fees, dues, and other payments 'for his own use and benefit'; but the statute set up for the first time a tuition fund into which he was obliged to pay one-third of all payments received for tuition; this was earmarked for the payment of tutors other than himself. While in other respects the principal retained his traditional autocracy, he was no longer to be rector of Gatcombe; an act of parliament was envisaged under which the advowson would be transferred from the university to Queen's, a charge of £150 p.a. payable to the hall being imposed on the incumbent's stipend. Under the settlement Queen's generously agreed to provide £300 a year for exhibitions at the hall.

With his fears of the hall's extinction removed, Moore at last felt free to resign. His last official act was to present several of his men for their degrees at the ceremony in the Sheldonian Theatre in July 1913. After he had pronounced the Latin formula of presentation, the vice-chancellor broke with precedent and, also in Latin, complimented him on completing almost fifty years as dean of degrees, assuring him that although he was leaving Oxford his vigorous hall would remain as a living witness to him.[17] Thenceforth he resided entirely at Canterbury, active as ever on the cathedral chapter, with the library as his special province. He died of a stroke at Chagford on 2 October 1916.

[17] For a full report see *Church Times* (11 July 1913).

IX

War and Post-War Expansion

I

THERE were some who hoped that S. L. Ollard, who had held the fort almost single-handed for a decade, would succeed Moore, but he had been too closely involved in the in-fighting of the past decade. In the event the choice of Queen's fell on 10 August 1913 on the Revd Herbert Henry Williams, MA. Nicknamed 'Burglar Bill' because of his stocky figure, bushy eyebrows, and cap pulled down over his forehead, he was a former Hastings exhibitioner of the college and had been philosophy fellow at Hertford since 1898. He had contributed articles, highly thought-of at the time, on ethics and on the will, to the *Encyclopaedia Britannica* (11th edn.). A reflective, determined man with a shrewd knowledge of affairs, he was widely respected in the university, and was almost immediately elected to hebdomadal council. He was rector (absentee) of Gatcombe until 1917, when he resigned from both the rectory and (formally) the principalship. He was re-elected principal, and re-instituted on 1 September 1917, but his resignation brought the act of parliament[1] separating the rectory from the principalship into effect.

When he was admitted to office on 29 September 1913, prospects for the hall looked brighter than for several years. The long deadlock with Queen's had been amicably ended; a principal and his wife were again occupying the lodgings; applications were gratifyingly on the upturn. If the staff he inherited was meagre—a part-time theology tutor and a senior tutor, G. R. Brewis, who covered the Pass subjects in popular demand—he had no difficulty in engaging a modern history tutor, and since Ollard had left for a country living, soon appointed an able former Greats pupil of his own, the Revd Leonard Hodgson (to become regius professor of divinity in 1944) as vice-principal. But these high hopes were quickly shown to be illusory.

---

[1] See above p. 102.

First, the hall's accounts were in chaos, and the university auditors, to whom the recent statute required him to submit them, declined to audit them. They murmured gloomily of possible insolvency. In fact, the first accounts of the hall to be published by the university (even these with caveats) covered the period 10 October 1913 to 31 December 1914. The buildings, too, for the upkeep and insurance of which he was personally responsible, were in a shocking state of disrepair. To meet the emergency Williams launched a public appeal in June 1914, persuading the always friendly visitor, Lord Curzon, to head it. Although some old members complained that he overstressed the hall's role as 'a poor man's college', he quickly raised little short of £2,000, much of it from colleges and sympathetic Oxford dons; Curzon himself contributed £100.

Secondly, the outbreak of World War I on 4 August 1914 had a paralysing effect on Oxford generally and in particular on its weaker societies. Although conscription was not introduced until 1916, practically all fit students volunteered for military or other service. The hall was not, as several colleges were, requisitioned as barracks, but everywhere admissions' lists were drastically cut. Williams had been expecting thirty-four freshmen in October 1914, but only seventeen turned up; before long several of these had disappeared. Numbers kept on falling; in September 1916 he noted, 'We shall have 14 men (mostly cripples) up next term.' Many rooms remained unoccupied. The financial impact on the hall, dependent as it was on room-rents and other charges, was daunting; Williams must have been grateful for the subvention he received from Gatcombe rectory.

With the general situation steadily deteriorating, he carried on throughout the war with characteristic imperturbability. He had to suspend his appeal in autumn 1914, and he later encouraged G. R. Brewis, who lacked passmen to teach, to take a schoolmastering post. He himself took steps to bring the accounts into order; since the hall had no bursary clerk, he arranged with the one at Hertford to keep an eye on them, with some discreet help from Mrs Williams. In 1915 he moved the JCR from the ground floor of the cottage (which Hodgson, who lived in the first floor, annexed) to a ground-floor room on Staircase 2. Although painfully aware that the hall lacked a bathroom (men bathed in tubs in their rooms, or hired one of the baths attached to the Merton Street swimming-pool), he could do nothing to remedy this deficiency. Still less had he the means to modernize the primitive latrine-hut, which stood behind shrubbery at the far right-hand corner of the quadrangle adjacent to the cottage (in which until 1915 undergraduates awaiting their turn after breakfast impatiently flicked through newspapers), and was popularly known as the 'South-East'. But in 1915/16, by using the money raised by his appeal, he carried out urgently needed repairs to the buildings, and installed electricity throughout and heating in the chapel and Old Library.

II

As the war drew to a close, conditions improved dramatically. Admissions in October 1918, in anticipation of the allied victory, shot up to twenty; in October 1919 they reached thirty-three, the total of junior members resident that term being eighty-five. More were recruited in each of the following terms until there were ninety-seven on the residents' list. Even more significant than these unprecedented numbers were the facts that, in contrast to the pre-war epoch, practically all the new intake were reading for honours, and the great majority were setting their sights at other professions than the priesthood. In the summer of 1919 Hodgson left to become dean of divinity at Magdalen, and the vice-principalship remained unfilled for many months. Earlier in that year, however, Williams had appointed A. B. Emden, a graduate of Lincoln College who had served as an able seaman in the Royal Navy, as tutor in modern history. In Michaelmas term he made him bursar as well, having decided that the greatly enlarged membership of the hall warranted the creation of the office. Meanwhile he was seeking financial support from the university, and in May 1920, much helped by the personal intervention of Lord Curzon, persuaded it to vote the hall a grant of £500 a year for three years.

Williams was nominated bishop of Carlisle in June 1920 and laid down the principalship on 1 October. The university, of which he was a leading figure, conferred on him an honorary DD by diploma; St Hilda's Hall (as it was still called) elected him, a former chairman of its council and a strenuous advocate of the 1920 statute admitting women to full membership of the university, as its first visitor. Although he had greatly strengthened the hall's position and its finances were on the mend, he remained deeply worried about its future. Rising numbers raised problems of their own; more resident tutors would be needed, and since most of the men were now reading for honours, their tuition would be much more expensive than that of passmen. He was also unhappy about the system under which the principal relied for his income on whatever surplus remained after all the hall's expenses, including tuition and the maintenance of the buildings, had been met. He voiced these doubts, and also his view that the best prospect for the hall lay in a reinforcement of the oversight and support the university had given it in recent years, in a memorandum he submitted before moving north to the Royal Commission which began investigating Oxford and Cambridge universities in 1919. His later career, as one of the church's most trusted and influential bishops (1920–46), lies outside these pages; but he was to serve the hall for many years as a trustee, gave it a valuable collection of books, and on his death (28 September 1961) bequeathed it the residue of his estate. He had been created Companion of Honour in 1945.[2]

III

As successor to Williams Queen's on 11 November 1920 elected the Revd Gerald Burton Allen, MA, BD, fellow and dean of Pembroke College, and senior proctor for the year. He was not its first choice; only when three or four others had declined the appointment (some pleading lack of private means) did it invite Allen to take over as acting principal, pending his formal election, at the beginning of Michaelmas term. Originally a Wadham man with no connection with Queen's, he had been with the YMCA in France during the war, and had also served as a chaplain with both the army and the air force. Like his predecessor, he was soon elected to hebdomadal council—a recognition of his effective proctorship. By contemporaries and undergraduates he was nicknamed 'Puffles'.

The community over which Allen presided for some eight years was a vigorous one. The salaried academic staff remained minute; by 1928 it still consisted of a vice-principal and two tutors (one of them in holy orders acting as chaplain). But it was already clear that

---

[2] See *SEHM* (1961–2), 36–8; also *The Times* (30 Sept. 1961), 12

the atmosphere was changing. First, Allen almost immediately appointed Emden to the vacant vice-principalship, leaving the internal management of the hall largely in his hands. Secondly, the number of junior members was steadily growing, from ninety-four in 1920 to 115 (including ten BAs) in 1928. A swollen influx was to be expected after the war, but its continuance was due not only to the fact that 'it offered a real Oxford life on more economical terms than the colleges could',[3] but also to the close corporate spirit which it was reputed to foster. In fact, the great majority of its undergraduates were men of modest means and family background. Almost all of them were reading for honours, their preferred schools being modern history, English, and (increasingly) modern languages. There were always a few reading theology, while one or two a year were beginning to opt for the natural sciences or the new school of PPE.

Several alterations and extensions to the buildings were carried out in Allen's principalship, some to remedy deficiencies but others to cater for the growing population. The driving force behind them was A. B. Emden, who also started the *St Edmund Hall Magazine* in 1920. In 1921 the dining-hall was enlarged, to seat seventy-five instead of forty-five, by the inclusion in it of the original entrance lobby. The kitchen of the principal's lodgings (the area now occupied by the college wine-cellar) was made the general kitchen of the hall, and a small portion of it was converted into a porter's lodge overlooking the entry from the main gate (previously the lodge had been inconveniently sited at the bottom of Staircase 2). A new, enlarged JCR was established on the ground floor of the north range. The undergraduate library, inaugurated in 1920 at the bottom of Staircase 1, was transferred in the following year to the large room on the first floor of the projecting east wing of the lodgings, which Allen had decided to dispense with. The top floor of this wing was adapted as undergraduate sets, and the ground floor brought into use in part as a bursary. These improvements were largely financed out of the annual grants which the hall continued to receive from the university.

With numbers high and steadily rising the hall's finances were beginning to acquire a firmer basis, and in 1923/4 it made unsuccessful efforts to obtain leases of houses in High Street

[3] See *OM* 46 (1927–8), 653.

(including the property at the corner of Queen's Lane) from Magdalen and Queen's. It had been more fortunate in 1922 in being able to purchase from Magdalen a narrow strip of garden east of the cottage, lying between the chapel and the rear of No. 48 High Street. In 1926, however, it embarked on a new building of its own, erecting a three-storey extension to the projecting east wing of the lodgings on a small plot of land bought the previous year from Magdalen—the site, in fact, of Airay's, or Link, Lodgings[4] in the seventeenth century (the ruins of which had to be pulled down). The ancient well in the middle of the quadrangle, the mouth of which had been sealed in the early seventeenth century, was rediscovered when the building yard for these works was being set up. The first floor of the new building (architect H. S. Rogers) was deployed as an extension of the undergraduate library, the bursary was moved to the ground floor, and bathrooms (the first the hall had known) were installed on the second floor. The building, which had cost some £6,620 (a quarter of this being subscribed by old members and friends), was formally opened in April 1927 by George, Viscount Cave, chancellor of the university and visitor of the hall. So far as is known, this was the first ceremonial visit by a chancellor to the hall.[5]

IV

There was a flurry of excitement for Allen and his vice-principal in January 1926 when there unexpectedly appeared in *The Times*[6] a letter signed by the vice-chancellor and a formidable group of heads of houses, arguing that the plans then being floated for the foundation in Oxford of an evangelical college, with the special purpose of assisting ordinands, would be far more usefully implemented by the endowment of St Edmund Hall, 'a venerable society [they averred] already devoted to this end'. The scare was fortunately short-lived. Allen rejected the gift-horse out of hand, and the promoters of the original scheme considered the hall's site too restricted; three years later they successfully launched St Peter's Hall (now College).

---

[4] See above p. 43.
[5] For an account of the opening see *SEHM* (1927), 12–15 (with frontispiece and photograph facing p. 12).
[6] For the correspondence see *The Times* (20 Jan. 1926). Cf. also E. H. F. Smith, *St Peter's: The Founding of an Oxford College* (Gerrards Cross, 1978), 21–2.

Only a few weeks after *The Times* letter, on 26 February 1926, the hall received (the university commissioners having completed their task) a new statute under the Oxford and Cambridge Universities Act 1923.[7] This modified the statute of 1913 in two important respects. First, it created a board of six trustees—the principal (chairman), one nominated by him, and two each elected by hebdomadal council and Queen's—charged with holding and administering the hall's property apart from the site and buildings, which continued to be vested in Queen's. As well as acknowledging that the hall was getting too big to be wholly in the charge of one man, this innovation took a modest step towards meeting Williams's plea that the university should assume an increasing responsibility for it. Secondly, it withdrew from the principal his traditional right to regard any surplus on the year's workings as his income, and instead (following a suggestion which Allen had put forward to the commissioners) assigned him a fixed stipend (£800 p.a. plus an entertainment allowance of £200 p.a.). As a corollary of this reform, all tuition fees were to be earmarked exclusively for the payment of tuition, and while the principal was still required to provide for the upkeep and insurance of the buildings, he was to do so out of the hall's general revenue. The statute also made provision for the setting up of a Building and Extension Fund and a special reserve fund, and for the admission of the hall to the Federated Superannuation Scheme for Universities if and when its finances permitted. The obligation of Queen's to contribute £300 p.a. for exhibitions was maintained.

In addition to this grant, the hall continued to receive £500 p.a. for its general purposes from the university throughout Allen's principalship. There was a steady strengthening of academic performance during this period; despite a high proportion of thirds and fourths, few years passed without a first being obtained in honour schools. With numbers on the increase corporate spirit ran high; it found expression in April 1925 in the foundation of an association for old members (the Aularian—later the St Edmund Hall—Association). Student societies and the sporting clubs were active; the morale of the latter was strengthened in 1920 when the hall began, for the first time, renting a ground from Wadham. A rugby football club, warranted by the growth in numbers, was

---

[7] *Statuta et Decreta Universitatis Oxoniensis* (1937), 19–29.

founded in 1922. There was recognition in the university that the hall was going through a period of vigorous development.[8]

In February 1928 Allen was appointed suffragan bishop of Sherborne, and his resignation as principal took effect from 6 May, the day of his consecration. He nevertheless continued to discharge the duties of principal until the end of June. His connection with the hall was to be resumed when he returned to Oxford in 1936 as canon of Christ Church and bishop of Dorchester, and for a number of years he served as one of its trustees. On his death in 1956 he bequeathed it a collection of books.

V

On 30 May 1928 Queen's elected the Revd George Bernard Cronshaw, MA, a senior fellow who was also bursar and chaplain, to the principalship. A genial man of 56, beloved by Queen's old members and for years a respected member of hebdomadal council, he had as treasurer and chairman of committee from 1910 to 1928 supervised important developments at the Radcliffe Infirmary (where he is still commemorated by a ward bearing his name). To Queen's the appointment seemed a natural promotion which also left the college free to seek a bursar with up-to-date skills in estate management and investment. It was also warmly welcomed in Oxford,[9] although in circles close to the hall there was acute disappointment that the vice-principal, who had played a decisive role in its recent progress, had been passed over, and uneasy fears that a brake would now be put on the vigorous expansionist policies he had been sponsoring.

Cronshaw was instituted in the dining-hall on 10 October. He had already, as was to be expected, taken over the bursarship from Emden. His health, however, hitherto robust, had gravely deteriorated, and it was evident at his institution that he was still a sick man. He was soon obliged to take to his bed, and although he dined in hall on St Edmund's day, that was his last public appearance. He died on 20 December, a few days after learning that he was to receive the freedom of the city. The exceptionally large crowd present at his funeral in St Mary's on 22 December bore witness to the affection and repute he enjoyed in Oxford.

[8] See *OM* 46 (1928), 653.
[9] See e.g. *OM* 46 (1928), 653.

X

Before and After World War II

I

ON 8 January 1929 the governing body of Queen's elected the vice-principal, Alfred Brotherston Emden, MA, to the principalship. As with his predecessors Williams and Allen, the college went, for what was to be its last appointment, outside the ranks of its own fellows, but its choice gave belated satisfaction to many who, recognizing that Emden had been the driving-force during Allen's reign, had been distressed by its preference for Cronshaw, himself said to have been a reluctant nominee, the previous year.

Only 41, the first layman and the first vice-principal to be appointed principal, Emden was a graduate of Lincoln College who, accepting an almost chance offer, had joined the hall as modern history tutor in Michaelmas term 1919 on being demobilized from the Royal Navy. For two or three years he seems to have been restive, prepared to consider invitations to move elsewhere, but soon identified himself with all the hall's activities as a vigorous and confident bursar and vice-principal. He also made himself an unrivalled investigator of its history, publishing in 1927 an exhaustive study[1] of its origins and development down to the mid-sixteenth century which at once brought him into the front rank of specialists in medieval intellectual life. His admission to office in the dining-hall by the vice-chancellor, to whom the provost of Queen's had presented him in the hall of Queen's (the last time this feature of the ceremony was to be enacted), inaugurated an energetic and individual principalship which only lost momentum as a result of World War II and subsequent ill health.

For his first decade Emden continued and extended the expansionist policies which had proved so successful under G. B. Allen when he was vice-principal. Like Allen, too, he played an

[1] *An Oxford Hall.*

active part in university business, serving on hebdomadal council continuously from 1935 to 1947. The hall when he took office was one of the poorest of Oxford societies, with capital investments barely exceeding £3,000 and heavily dependent on annual grants of £500 from the university chest, £300 (for exhibitions) from Queen's, and £150 from Gatcombe rectory[2] (a charge the surrender of which he sternly declined to consider). Administratively it was run on a shoe-string; until the late thirties the bursary was staffed by a single, elderly clerk who was responsible for preparing all bills and accounts, and for keeping records. For the larger part of his reign Emden had no private secretary, writing most of his letters in longhand and calling on the bursary clerk for those which needed to be typed and copied. On becoming principal he at once reassumed the bursarship, which Cronshaw had obliged him to relinquish, and retained it until 1949. Throughout he kept a tight rein on expenditure in every department, and by efficient house-keeping was responsible for the consistently healthy condition of the hall's modest finances. In 1932 he instituted an Endowment and Extension Fund, based on an appeal to old members, and in 1938 merged this with an Endowment appeal addressed to the wider public. By the time of his retirement in 1951 the combined funds had reached a total of some £23,000.

As in previous generations, the hall still offered its members, and deliberately sought to maintain, a more economical, if also more frugal, life than the colleges. High spending was discouraged; on Mondays, for example, the butteryman brought his book to the vice-principal, and students who were found to have exceeded the accepted norm of beer consumption were warned, rebuked, or penalized. Its comparative cheapness made the hall attractive to many, especially to the ordinands and prospective schoolteachers who still formed a higher-than-average proportion of its members, and in part explains why, in the recession of the early thirties when some colleges were experiencing difficulty in filling their entry lists, the number of its undergraduates (a vital statistic for a society dependent on its receipts from junior members) rose from 101 in Michaelmas term 1929 to 146 (including sixty freshmen) in Michaelmas term 1938. The disquiet which this enlargement excited in some quarters found official expression in 1937, when

---

[2] See above p. 102

the university made the renewal of its yearly subsidy conditional on the total number of undergraduates in residence not rising above 150.

In addition to comparative inexpensiveness the hall's popularity in the thirties with grammar and direct-grant schools, and with minor to middling public schools, owed much to their recognition of its infectious corporate spirit. This found an outlet in runs of successes both in sport and in amateur dramatics which added to the confidence of its junior members. Illustrations were a famous bump supper which was held in the quadrangle (the dining-hall was too small) in May 1930,[3] and the comment of James Agate, the widely read dramatic critic, that St Edmund Hall had become 'the green room of Oxford'. Emden fostered this spirit with skill and enthusiasm, showing exceptional personal concern for his under-graduates and, although always keeping a distance, involving himself in their activities. One of his achievements was to start renting playing-fields, for games other than cricket, in the Parks. A benevolent paternalist, he used his influence on occasion to ensure that the right junior members were promoted to the right offices, and was unique among college heads in periodically attending and addressing meetings of the junior common room. The choice of commoners lay entirely in his hands, and his wishes prevailed in the election of the handful of exhibitioners. It has been fairly observed that in these pre-war years the hall had much of the close corporate atmosphere, and also of the limitations, of a small public school, and that his style resembled that of a loved and revered headmaster. Like some headmasters but few heads of houses, he drew to himself from his undergraduates (all of whom he regularly entertained to breakfast, lunch, or tea) an extraordinary combination of awe and devotion, even hero-worship.

Emden's first vice-principal (1929–37) was an able modern historian from Hertford, the Revd J. S. Brewis. When he moved elsewhere after getting married (a state Emden deemed, somewhat unhistorically, incompatible with the office), he appointed the Revd J. N. D. Kelly, a graduate of Glasgow University and Queen's, whom he had invited to the hall as chaplain and tutor in theology and philosophy in 1935. In addition the hall relied, as in the twenties, on a small band of salaried tutors—three in 1929, six in

[3] For a dramatic photograph see *SEHM*(1930), facing p. 6.

1938—three or four lecturers in receipt of a small retaining fee, and a range of outside tutors; the tuition fees paid to lecturers and outside tutors were markedly lower than the rates generally accepted in the colleges. The staple subjects catered for were theology, modern history, English, modern languages (unusually for the time, the hall maintained a full-time tutor in French), and chemistry. There were still one or two men studying for Greats, and a firm start was being made with PPE; there was also a handful of passmen. The tutors were able teachers, and included such an outstanding scholar as H. J. Hunt, later to be known for his work on Balzac. The hall scored several academic successes in the thirties: in 1932, for example, three firsts were obtained in final honour schools, and four Heath Harrison travelling scholarships in modern languages. These results were all the more impressive because the hall, which offered no open scholarships, held its exhibition and principal entrance examination in the Easter vacation, when the colleges had already taken their pick of the talent available; apart from occasional stars, its intake was in general intellectually mediocre.

The position of the tutors compared unfavourably with that of college fellows. Not only were their salaries well below the normal standard, but they had no pension rights, although Emden promised they would come in due course. Further, until the passing of new statutes in 1937, they had none of the constitutional rights of fellows; they were appointed, and could be dismissed, by the principal, who also settled with each the financial terms of his appointment. On admission they had to take an oath, without parallel in colleges, to obey the principal 'in all things lawful and honourable'. They also lacked the usual high table facilities, since undergraduates dined with them at the top table (seniors and juniors shared an identical meal), and had no common room of their own. It was Emden's practice to invite them, often with leading undergraduates, to coffee in his lodgings after dinner; and it was in his drawing-room that formal meetings of the principal and fellows were held. Although the work-load of Oxford dons was in general heavier than it became after World War II, that of the tutors of the hall was excessive by any standards: twenty to twenty-five required tutorial hours a week were not unusual. These disabilities became increasingly anomalous and irksome as the hall expanded and approximated, in its general life, more and more to a college, and could not bode well for the future. In 1935, for example, its chaplain, a philosophical theologian of rare calibre (A. M. Farrer: author, it should be recorded, of the Latin 'Hymn of St Edmund'), felt obliged to move to one of the colleges because his salary was insufficient to support a married man.

II

An obstacle to the hall's expansion in the late twenties and thirties (indeed, for the rest of the period coverd by this book, and beyond) was an acute shortage of accommodation. In Michaelmas term 1928, for example, it possessed only twenty-five sets of rooms for an undergraduate population of 105. As a result it became necessary in most years to relax the rule that every junior member should have at least one year's residence in hall. Emden, who on taking office had arranged for two students to be housed in the attics of his lodgings (he was a bacheor), made determined and successful efforts to overcome this difficulty. First, in 1930 he negotiated with Magdalen College a twenty-one-year lease of No. 48 High Street (now No. 8 Staircase), thus bringing the hall down to the High for the first time since its relinquishment of White Hall and St Hugh (or Grammar) Hall in the fifteenth century.[4] This house, with the ramshackle building projecting behind it, was linked up with the patch of garden and open space east of the cottage purchased from the college in 1922.[5] Then in the long vacation of 1932 he secured leases, again from Magdalen and for twenty-one years, of the adjacent houses Nos. 46 and 47 High Street (occupying the site of White Hall). These three houses provided accommodation for some twenty-five undergraduates, as well as a lecture-room, a tutor's teaching-room, a set for a resident don, and sorely needed bathrooms and changing-rooms.

Finally, the completion of the quadrangle was made possible by the purchase in 1933 of a long, narrow strip of land on its south side from Queen's, and of a much smaller plot at the upper end of the garden behind No. 46 High Street from Magdalen. The demolition of an unsightly red-brick shed used as a storehouse by Messrs Minty, the furniture dealers, which had for years occupied the Queen's site, was at once taken in hand, and work on an entirely new residential range (architect R. Fielding Dodd) started.

---

[4] See above p. 25.
[5] See above p. 108.

13. Watched by Principal Emden (right) and the architect, Archbishop Lang blesses the Canterbury Building

The complete building, which was closely modelled externally on the cottage (*c.*1600), was ready for occupation by Michaelmas term 1934, and was declared open and blessed by the archbishop of Canterbury (Cosmo Gordon Lang) on 10 October.[6] It was named the Canterbury Building because (as a Latin inscription by A. M. Farrer indicates) its opening coincided with the 700th anniversary of the consecration of St Edmund of Abingdon as archbishop. It provided nine sets of rooms. The total expenditure which the completion of the quadrangle entailed was £10,000; to help the hall to meet this, the university chest provided a loan of £5,000. To replace the now dismantled 'South-East'[7] a shed containing a more commodious set of WCs was constructed to the east of the chapel.

During these years Emden not only thoroughly restored the hall's existing buildings, but carried out certain important modifications of them. First, in 1931 a sacristy on the ground floor and an organ-loft were added to the chapel, and Penton's library, with its gallery, was extended northwards above the former, the dummy windows in the west-facing façade being at last opened up. This involved the purchase from New College for £150 of a minute segment of its garden. Secondly, when in 1932 the Welsh slates then covering the south-facing roof of the north range of the quadrangle were replaced with Stonesfield slates, the unsightly two-light dormers[8] placed there in 1844 were reconstructed as oak-framed windows of four lights (as portrayed in the 1814 Ackermann print by F. Pugin). Thirdly, in the same year Room 2 of Staircase 1, with good reason believed to have been Thomas Hearne's study,[9] was restored as a general-purposes room bearing his name. Finally, in the summer of 1934 two bedrooms over the north end of the dining-hall were dismantled, and replaced by a gallery equipped with a table and benches for some fourteen overflow diners.

III

When opening the Canterbury Building in October 1934, arch-bishop Lang had disclosed that it was the intention of Queen's, after some 370 years of tutelage, to grant the hall complete

---

[6] For a description of the opening, with photographs of Emden addressing the gathering and the archbishop blessing the building, see *SEHM* (1934), 24–30.

[7] See above p. 105.

[8] For a photograph of these, and an article describing the change, see *SEHM* (1932), 18–19.　　　　　　　　　　　　　　　[9] See above p. 55.

independence. This historic decision in large measure reflected altered circumstances; the principalship had long ceased to be the attraction it had once been to fellows of the college, and there was also wide recognition in the university that the hall had reached a size and standing which made independence appropriate. But it also owed much both to the persuasions of Emden himself and to the view taken by the provost, the well-known New Testament scholar B. H. Streeter (a close friend of Emden), and a group of younger fellows (for example, O. S.—later Lord—Franks) that the traditional relationship had become obsolete. Its implementation made new statutes necessary, for Queen's planned not only to abandon the right to appoint the principal, but also (subject to certain safeguards) to divest itself of the site and buildings. These statutes were submitted to both the college and hebdomadal council, but they in fact mirrored Emden's own conception of what an academical hall should be in modern times. They were brought before congregation in February–March 1937.

The first statute provided the hall with a new constitution replacing that of 1926.[10] This raised the number of trustees from six to ten, four of them to be representative of the university chest, Queen's, the fellows, and the association of old members respectively, and the remaining six to be elected by the principal and the other trustees (which effectively left the initiative in choosing them with the principal). Under the statute the principal and trustees shared responsibility for investments and financial administration generally, including the settlement of salaries for academic and other staff. Elections to the principalship were entrusted to the trustees. Secondly, while it was prominently stated that 'the principal shall have charge of the hall', and that its governance in all its departments should be vested in him, it was also provided that the fellows, as the tutors were now designated for the first time, should collaborate with him in matters affecting internal administration and educational policy. Thirdly, in order to avoid the necessity for periodical transferences of investments whenever new trustees were appointed, it was arranged that all the hall's real and personal property, with the exception of the site and buildings, should be vested in the university as custodian trustee, the trustees acting as managing trustees.

[10] See above p. 109.

When the statute was introduced in congregation, it met with opposition which Emden had not anticipated; there were those in the university who had looked for much more far-reaching reforms. H. M. Last, Camden professor of ancient history, took exception[11] to what he considered the excessive measure of autocracy still reserved to the principal, which, he argued, would deter men of ability and character from seeking fellowships in a society which allowed them little of the independence taken for granted by fellows of colleges. Emden immediately held discussions with Last, and several agreed amendments were submitted to congregation on 7 March; the statute so amended was passed on 4 May.[12] Although Emden yielded few points of substance to Last, he at least agreed to the excision of a clause which effectively gave the principal a veto on all decisions purporting to be made by the principal and fellows. Even as amended that statute left the principal with much greater say in administering the hall, and the fellows markedly less, than was customarily enjoyed by heads and fellows of colleges. Emden frankly avowed that, while anxious to limit the quasi-monarchical powers of the principal, he did not wish to do so at the cost of obliterating the historic features differentiating ancient halls from colleges: it had 'been deemed [i.e. by himself] preferable that the hall should remain the oldest surviving hall rather than become the youngest of the colleges'.[13]

Under the second statute[14] arrangements were made for the transfer of the site and buildings, which had been vested in Queen's since 1557, together with parcels of land acquired for the hall subsequently, to the Official Trustee for Charity Lands. It might have seemed more natural to vest this real property with the new trustees, but that would have made a fresh conveyance necessary whenever there was a change among the trustees. In so divesting itself of its ancient freehold Queen's nevertheless stipulated for the retention of the right of reversion in the event of the hall's ever ceasing to be an independent self-governing institution for the education of male students, barring exceptional circumstances such as war, civil strife, or epidemic; it also bound the hall not to

---

[11] For a brief but accurate report of his intervention, see *OM* 67 (1936–7), 461–3.

[12] See *OUG* 67 (1936–7), 445–53 (original text of the statute); 500 (amendments); 543–51 (statute as finally accepted).

[13] See *SEHM* (1937), 7, 21.

[14] See text in *OUG* 67 (1936–7), 461–3.

increase the height of its buildings, nor to prejudice its reversionary interest by mortgaging the land or buildings for sums exceeding £1,500. For its part the college agreed to continue to pay to the principal for 15 years the annual sum of £300 for the provision of exhibitions for students.

The new statutes came into operation on being approved by the king in council on 21 December 1937. The trustees appointed included two, Sir Arthur C. McWatters, secretary to the university chest, and Douglas (later Sir) Veale, university registrar, whose counsel was to prove invaluable over many years; the fellows elected the vice-principal to be their representative. The principal and fellows soon used their new powers to elect three honorary fellows, the first in the hall's history. They were a former principal, H. H. Williams, a former vice-principal, S. L. Ollard, and the most distinguished alumnus from the pre-war decade, J. W. C. Wand, archbishop of Brisbane, later to become bishop of London. The fact that all three were clerics reflected the older complexion of the hall. On 16 November (St Edmund's day) next year Emden launched, with wide-ranging sponsorship, an Endowment Appeal, merging with it the Endowment and Extension appeal which he had founded in 1932. He stressed that, now that the hall had secured its independence, it was warranted in appealing for support to a wider audience than its old members.

In autumn 1939 Emden and the trustees began, and in 1941 completed, negotiations for the purchase from Magdalen of the residue of the lease, due to expire in the year 2005, of the Masonic buildings,[15] situated behind Nos. 49, 50, 51, and 52 High Street and abutting on the open area behind No. 8 Staircase. This complex pile, erected in 1906, covered some 11,000 square feet and included a large and a small dining-hall, a masonic temple, and ancillary rooms, and had been let by the college on a ninety-nine-year lease. For the moment nothing could be done with the property, for not only was it occupied by the Royal Army Medical Corps in 1939, but the head-lease was encumbered with three conterminous subleases held by masonic lodges in the city and entitling them to make use of the premises on numerous days in the year. Nevertheless the hall considered the expenditure incurred, £6,500, a prudent investment in the future.

---

[15] See *SEHM* (1941), 41.

IV

As World War II approached, it was confidently expected in the university that, on its outbreak, men would be called to military service at the age of 18, student numbers being thereby reduced to a trickle. Plans were accordingly made for appropriating colleges to other purposes: the hall was to be taken over by the women dons and students of Westfield College, London, on its evacuation from the capital. When it was announced that the call-up age was to be 20, and that medical and engineering students, and other classes of scientists, were to be deferred, the university and colleges had to make last-minute arrangements for the reception of the normal complement of freshmen and of numbers of second- and third-year men.

The hall found itself able, at the eleventh hour, to extricate itself from its compact with Westfield. Throughout the war, while most colleges were partially or wholly taken over by government or were housing undergraduates from other societies as well as their own, it was almost alone in having no other occupants than its own tutors and students. The number of undergraduates on its books in Michaelmas terms 1939, 1940, and 1941 was ninety-four, ninety-five, and 110; in addition there were always a few BAs. Even when the call-up age was progressively lowered to 18, the gap was largely filled by the institution of six-month courses for RAF and Royal Signals Corps cadets in 1941, and in 1943 for RN cadets; these had been selected as potential university material, were shared out among the colleges by the registry, and were matriculated as members of the university. Numbers were therefore fully maintained in Michaelmas term 1942 with a record intake of seventy-one freshmen; although they declined somewhat after that, there were eighty-two and eighty-seven undergraduates, including probationer cadets, in residence in Michaelmas terms 1943 and 1944 respectively.

Unlike most colleges, the hall retained the services of most of its senior members during the war since they fell into the age-group designated as 'reserved'. The sole exception was the modern history fellow (G. D. Ramsay), who was commissioned in the RAF in 1941; the Revd Professor Norman Sykes, of Westfield College (which had found refuge in St Peter's Hall), substituted for him for several terms. Emden himself, however, was appointed commanding officer of the Oxford University Naval Division, with the rank of Lieutenant Commander (Sp.). He had worked behind the scenes to secure its formation, and his duties in connection with it absorbed most of his time and energies in 1943 and 1944. He nevertheless found time to follow the fortunes of, and maintain a vast, handwritten correspondence with, hundreds of aularians serving with the forces. The other fellows, in addition to their tutorial and administrative duties, were all involved in part-time war service of various kinds. Although the total of undergraduates in residence at any one time was well below the levels that had become normal at the hall, the facts that their turnover was rapid, and that the courses for service cadets covered the whole year except for two weeks, meant that the tutorial burden on fellows and lecturers was continuous and exceptionally heavy.

The hall (other colleges too) was thus able to maintain throughout the war a vigorous, if reduced, life of a kind which had never been anticipated in the late thirties. While a small minority of undergraduates studied for the traditional honour schools, the great majority worked for the special 'honour sections' or shortened courses which were devised for the emergency. For games the colleges generally paired off with neighbours; the hall's sporting clubs formed an appropriate, successful alliance with those of Queen's. The debating and other societies kept up lively meetings, and officers were regularly elected for the junior common room; in 1943, because of the transitory residence of most undergraduates, a medical student (C. J. Starey) had to be persuaded by the authorities to serve as president for a second year. Conditions were restricted with rationing in force and the black-out rigidly observed. The absence of most of the domestic staff on war service made it necessary to require undergraduates to make their beds and keep their rooms tidy; the results were distinctly patchy. All residents had fire-watching duties assigned them, and although Oxford escaped bombing the air-raid sirens frequently sounded as hostile aircraft swept overhead on their way to the industrial Midlands.

There were brighter moments in the summers of 1940 and 1941, before the long vacations were crowded out by courses for probationer cadets, when a forestry-camp was organized in Somerset and a harvesting-camp in the Cotswolds for under-graduates awaiting, or not eligible for, call-up. A historic occasion was the holding by the bishops (Anglican) of England, Scotland, and Wales, by the invitation of the principal, of their annual meeting at the hall, Lambeth palace having been made unusable by bomb damage, from 30 June to 7 July 1941.[16] From time to time dons and students would gather round the vice-principal's wireless to listen to the sombre war news or be braced by Churchill's speeches; and once or twice a small crowd in chapel stumbled through the Te Deum to celebrate the eventual triumphs of the allied armies.

V

At dinner on VE day (8 May 1945) there was free beer in the hall, and the panelling behind the high table displayed the flags of Great Britain, the United States, and the Soviet Union. After all the excitements were over, the signs of wartime preparedness—static water-tanks, protective concrete walling at strategic points, girders underpinning the dining-hall and planking shielding the chapel east window, black-out curtains and blinds—were all removed with astonishing celerity. Preparations were made for the resumption of normal conditions. But it was not forgotten that some sixty-five aularians, a significant proportion of the hall's 1,600 past and present members, had laid down their lives. Their names were inscribed (lettering by H. Tyson-Smith) on the west-facing south side of the screen separating the chapel and the antechapel, and this was dedicated by the bishop of London (J. W. C. Wand) on 25 June 1949 at a service held in connection with the annual reunion.[17]

The rush back was slow in beginning. In Michaelmas term 1945 there were 100 undergraduates and graduate students in residence. For the same term in 1946 and 1947, however, the numbers shot up to 182 and 247. These inflated figures (the total had risen to 262 by 1949) were brought about, not by the admission of exaggerated numbers of freshmen, but by the return of men on demobilization to complete their interrupted courses, and also by the switches of government policy in 'deferring' men for national service (which continued for several years). The facts that the undergraduates were so numerous, and that often little notice was given of the date of their return from the forces, created acute problems both of tuition

---

[16] See *SEHM* (1941), 43–4 (article with pictures).
[17] See *SEHM* (1949), 20–3.

and of accommodation. The vice-principal had to expend much time either in attempting to engage tutors, especially in increasingly popular subjects like politics and economics, or else in bicycling around Oxford trying to book lodgings for men who had suddenly announced their imminent return. Many had no opportunity of residing in hall at all, while others could be allocated a room for only one or at most two terms. The only additional accommodation which could be brought into play was a couple of undergraduate sets and a small dispensary (grandly designated Staircase 11) at the back of No. 46 High Street, which had been placed at the disposal of Messrs Minty in 1933 to compensate it for the loss of its repairs shop when the Canterbury Building was erected.

Despite chaotic conditions, this was something of a halcyon period. Having served in the war or on national service, the majority of students were more mature, experienced, and independent than their pre-war predecessors. They included a sprinkling of able men who were to achieve distinction in either public or academic life (e.g. N. R. Wylie, to be solicitor-general for Scotland and then lord advocate; C. Grayson, to become professor of Italian and FBA), or as leaders in broadcasting or journalism (e.g. Robin Day, of the BBC, and Peter Nichols, of *The Times*). The composition of the undergraduate body began to change, with a decreasing proportion aiming at the ministry or the teaching profession, and many more seeking careers in business, the public service, or the law. The social mix was also becoming noticeably wider, and for the first time a fair number of students were married. Performance in schools fluctuated, but in June 1950 the principal was able to report at an old members' gathering that five firsts had been obtained in final examinations, while the presidents of both the Union Society and the OU Athletics Club were aularians. Nevertheless, the official view of the university obstinately remained the nineteenth-century one that the hall's *raison d'être* (like that of St Peter's and St Catherine's) was to be an economical society for students of modest means, and on the recommendation of the Central Scholarship Committee its undergraduates were accorded somewhat smaller maintenance grants from public funds than those of the colleges.[18] This anomaly, as it had become, was the subject of vigorous protests by the hall—the

[18] For some figures and comments see e.g. *Isis*, No. 1007 (Jan. 1947), 8.

vice-principal arguing strenuously before the committee that in the post-war world the colleges were bound to be less expensive than relatively unendowed societies—and within a few years was removed.

VI

For most of the war the hall had been served by a single clerk in the bursary, the assistant Emden had engaged in the late thirties having been soon called up, but in 1947 the growing volume of business necessitated the appointment of a second member of staff; next year he was accorded the title of secretary of the hall. In 1945 the hall at last applied for membership of the Federated Superannuation System for Universities; its application was accepted, and from 1946 the fellows (the principal firmly refused to join) enjoyed the pension arrangements normal throughout the university. In December 1946 the decision was taken to break new ground by appointing a stockbroker; he was Sir Frank Newson-Smith, of the firm of Newson-Smith and Co., financial advisers to the university. In June 1949 the principal and trustees agreed that, in view of a recent statute authorizing the university to invest in equities, the hall's investment policy should be brought into line with that of the university; while in March 1951 they accepted and put forward to the privy council a scheme allowing them as trustees to pool the investments held by the hall's trust funds; the scheme was modelled on one recently adopted for St Hugh's College.

The tutorial problems created by swollen numbers after the war, and also by the interest undergraduates were showing in the newer subjects, called for urgent action, and to meet them the hall expanded somewhat its meagre academic staff. In addition to the existing fellows in theology and philosophy, chemistry, modern history, English literature, and French, a second fellow in modern history and politics (Revd J. McManners: he was also to be chaplain) was elected in 1949, and in 1950 a fellow for the first time in geography (C. F. W. R. Gullick); this latter was becoming, and for many years was to remain, a major subject of study at the hall. In several fields, however, a solution was found by the multiplication of lecturerships carrying, in addition to tuition fees, somewhat arbitrarily calculated retainers. In 1950/1 the hall could boast of official lecturers in jurisprudence, zoology, Spanish,

German, English language, Italian, mathematics, English literature, and economics. The list bears witness to the special interest the hall took at this time, and was to continue to take, in the honour schools of modern languages and of English language and literature.

Two projects which were much discussed in these immediate post-war years, but which came to nothing (for the time being at any rate), concerned the Masonic buildings[19] and the adjacent parish church of St Peter-in-the-East. Emden and Kelly together thoroughly inspected the former in summer 1946, soon after the derequisitioning of the premises by the military authorities, but were forced to conclude that no practical use could be made of them by the hall so long as the masonic lodges retained subleases entitling them to make periodical use of them. Negotiations to persuade the lodges to dispose of the subleases came to nothing, and so the hall let the buildings to Burton's Dairies, Headington, for ten years, to be used as a restaurant known as The Forum. In this a ball, the first full-scale one the hall had ever put on, was held in June 1947. In 1950, however, the hall succeeded in obtaining from Magdalen College a twenty-one-year lease of Nos. 49–52 High Street, fronting the Masonic buildings, and also a renewal of its lease of Nos. 46–8 High Street. At the same time the trustees approved a plan for converting the residential portions of the former houses (Magdalen had kept the shops on the street to itself) to college rooms which had been prepared by Fielding Dodd and Stevens, architects.

With St Peter-in-the-East the hall had had ties since medieval times, since its members had attended services there down to 1682, and Merton College, the patron of the living, was now keen that it should assume responsibility for the church, agreeing to appoint the nominee of the principal as vicar. Pressure was several times brought on Kelly, both by the hall and by the diocesan authorities, to accept the benefice while remaining vice-principal and fellow. The hope was that such an arrangement would eventually lead to the hall's taking over the church and churchyard, and also the substantial vicarage in South Parks Road; various plans for the use of the latter were discussed. After much searching of the heart he declined, pointing out that any connection so formed would be a

---

[19] See above p. 120.

merely personal one and, if he were to develop an active parochial ministry (as he would feel bound to do), could lead to divided loyalties. The project in this form was dropped, but in summer 1947 Merton, on Emden's nomination, appointed a graduate student of the hall in holy orders as vicar of the parish.

In 1950 fresh prospects were opened for the hall by a windfall benefaction which the university steered in its direction. When M. Antonin Besse, of Aden, gave Oxford £1m. for the foundation of a new graduate college, to be called St Antony's, in which a proportion of places might be reserved for French scholars, he was at the same time persuaded (Douglas Veale, the registrar and trustee of the hall, played a key role in this) to place a further sum of £250,000 at the disposal of the university to enable existing colleges to co-operate with him in realizing this objective. In May 1950 congregation approved the allocation of capital grants of varying sizes to eight of the less-well-endowed societies—Exeter, Lincoln, Wadham, Pembroke, Worcester and Keble Colleges, St Peter's Hall and St Edmund Hall—for the purpose of improving accommodation, endowing teaching, and offering places to French students. The sum assigned to the hall was £38,000, much the largest benefaction it had ever received. While the provision of scholarships for Frenchmen was given priority, more than half of the money (£25,000) was earmarked by the principal and trustees for the enlargement of residential accommodation. It was the availability of the Besse fund which emboldened the hall in June 1950 to plan the conversion of Nos. 49–52 High Street to student rooms.

VII

During the post-war quinquennium Emden suffered from periodical bouts of ill health. He believed himself to be suffering from serious heart-trouble, and it is certain that he was the victim of severe nervous tension which incapacitated him from time to time. Enforced absences every few months, including occasional stays in a nursing-home, obliged him to devolve on the vice-principal not only bursarial functions (for example, the engagement of domestic staff), but also, for shorter or longer spells, the management of official correspondence, the selection of tutors, and the inter-viewing of applicants for admission. He had resigned in 1945, on doctor's advice, his chairmanship of the Oxford University Appointments Committee and several school governorships, and did not seek re-election to hebdomadal council when his current term of office expired. In summer 1949 he decided, on health grounds even more than because of the mounting administrative burden, to give up the bursarship, and with the trustees' consent appointed as half-time domestic bursar a friend (C. H. Jenner) who had recently retired from a similar full-time position in a public school.

It was a further strain on him that in these years his relations with the fellows, now more numerous than before the war, and also more independent and more impatient of the limited role assigned to them under the 1937 statutes, were becoming increasingly uneasy. In 1949, in a half-hearted attempt to allay their dissatisfaction, he agreed to the appointment of a second fellow (the senior tutor: Revd R. Fletcher) as a trustee in addition to the vice-principal. There was a flare-up between him and the fellows in the winter of 1949–50 when they demanded that the seventeenth-century library over the chapel, which was kept locked and hardly ever used, should be placed at their disposal as a common room; the lack of one was a severe inconvenience, and placed them at a disadvantage as compared with college fellows. After a period of storm-in-teacup squabbling the matter was amicably resolved, and from mid-January 1950 the fellows (who had used the Hearne Room for lunch for several years) had a gracious common room of their own, with a democratically elected steward and an embryonic constitution. At Emden's suggestion the trustees allocated one-half of a legacy of £1,000 left by his friend Graham Maurice Hamilton to the hall for the purchase of furniture for it. Characteristically, Emden insisted that meetings of the principal and fellows should continue to be held in the drawing-room of his lodgings (the fellows would have chosen neutral ground), and often preferred to retire there with a party of undergraduates after dinner rather than join the fellows in the Old Library.

On the eve of Trinity term 1951 he gave notice to the trustees and to the fellows that he planned to retire as from 31 July. He was only 63, but in spite of persistent ill health his retirement was to prove unexpectedly long (longer indeed than his principalship) and exceptionally rich in scholarly achievement. Among other works he completed and published, single-handed, magisterial registers of

the alumni of Oxford down to 1540 and of Cambridge down to
1500 which both transformed the historian's knowledge of the
universities in the medieval period, and won him the applause of
the learned world. At his retirement he presented the hall with
drawings, engravings, historical collections, and plate, and in
subsequent years lavished further gifts on it. When he died on
8 January 1979, he bequeathed the college (as it had become) the
residue of his estate, amounting to over £400,000. As well as being
the principal who freed it from the leading strings of Queen's, he
thus became the hall's most munificent single benefactor. His ashes
were interred, as he had requested, under the pavement of the
antechapel before the two war memorials.[20]

[20] For obituaries see *Proceedings of the British Academy* 65 (1979), 641–52
(by R. B. Pugh: with good head-and-shoulders photograph); *SEHM* (1978–9), 20–3
(by the present writer).

XI

From Hall to Mixed College

I

ON 22 June 1951 the trustees, with the support of the fellows, who had met previously and voted unanimously for him, elected the present writer as principal. He had been vice-principal since 1937, had recently published his first book and taken his DD, and was university lecturer (CUF) in patristic studies; he was also a canon of Chichester. He was the first, and as events were to show the only, principal appointed under the procedure set up by the 1937 statutes. At his institution on 11 October the traditional ceremony had to be modified (he had himself rearranged it, and redrafted the Latin formulae) since Queen's was no longer the presenting body. It was held entirely in the dining-hall, where he was presented to the vice-chancellor (Sir Maurice Bowra) by the presiding trustee (bishop G. B. Allen).

Kelly was 42 when he took office; his principalship of twenty-eight years was to be longer than that of any of his predecessors except Edward Moore (forty-nine years), who was not subject to a fixed retirement age. There was a break in it of several months in 1966/7, when he was incapacitated by serious illness (being obliged to resign from the vice-chancellorship, to which he had been admitted in September 1966). These were crowded and exciting years which witnessed radical changes in the hall's constitution, a spectacular enlargement of its site and buildings, and an increase in the number, variety, and classes of its fellowship which transformed its academic effectiveness. From the start it silently abandoned the role, accepted since the eighteenth century and sedulously cultivated in the nineteenth and early twentieth, of providing a full Oxford education at more economical rates than the colleges. This had been on the way out in the immediate post-war quinquennium, but had been made obsolete (as Keble, St Catherine's, and St Peter's were also quick to perceive) by the public funding of student grants and university lecturerships. As a result of all these developments it was able to take its place, no longer an anomalous and partly dependent society, in the mainstream of university life.

II

High on the agenda of the new principal and his small band of colleagues was the transformation of the hall into a college, i.e. an incorporated society which could control its own destiny and in the government of which head and fellows would participate equally. There was a romantic charm in being 'the only surviving medieval hall', but an academic community which could not own property directly and in which key decisions were taken by non-fellow trustees was not likely in modern Oxford to attract, still less retain, scholars of ability and independence. The reaction of Queen's and the university, when sounded privately by the principal shortly after he had taken office, was encouraging; any doubts the trustees had were dissipated when the privy council rejected their pooling scheme[1] in January 1952 on the ground that a hall was not an institution recognized by the Universities and Colleges (Trusts) Act 1943. It was known, however, that the recently retired principal was hostile to the change, and his enormous influence with old members could easily have swung them against it. The tactic adopted, therefore, was to rectify the position of the fellows immediately within the existing framework, and to seek incorporation when the moment seemed ripe. It was a tactic which paid off, for within three years Emden had been converted into an enthusiast for reform.

The hall's constitution was thus revised in two stages. First, an interim statute[2] amending the 1937 statutes was enacted in congregation in Michaelmas term 1952. Its salient provision was that all the fellows should be *ipso facto* trustees, but it also ensured that the non-fellow trustees should not have a preponderant vote. The second stage was completed on 15 February 1957 when the queen in council, in response to a petition from the visitor (the earl of Halifax) and the principal, granted the hall a charter making its head, fellows, and scholars a corporate body for the education of 'men who are members of the university of Oxford'. The new college (the ancient name had been deliberately retained) was

[1] See above p. 125.
[2] For the text see *OUG* 83 (1952–3), 234–6.

empowered not only to take over all the hall's property, including the land currently vested in the Official Trustee for Charity Lands (without prejudice however to the reversionary and other rights of Queen's), but also to acquire and hold property on its own. Two schedules were annexed to the charter: the first constituted the present principal and eleven fellows as the first governing body, while the second set out the new statutes, fourteen in number. These had been drafted by B. G. Campbell,[3] of the university registry, in consultation with the principal, and had been approved by the fellows. They conformed to the usual pattern of college statutes, and, while fulsomely stressing the 'pre-eminence' and initiative of the principal, made it clear that the hall was now an autonomous corporation in which all decisions were to be taken by the principal and fellows jointly. In future the election of their head should rest, as at the colleges generally, with the official fellows. The university had already passed a decree in Trinity term 1956 agreeing to recognize the hall, if and when the charter was granted, as a full college possessing all the privileges and responsibilities of colleges.

The new statutes came into operation immediately, but on the afternoon of 6 June 1958 Prince Philip, duke of Edinburgh, paid the first royal visit to the college (as it had been for some sixteen months) and, in the presence of the visitor, the vice-chancellor, and an enormous crowd of senior and junior members assembled in the quadrangle, handed the charter to the principal.[4] Later in the year the junior common room, which had independently decided that the historic constitutional change called for commemoration, presented the college with the altar-piece by Ceri Richards (1903–71) depicting the Supper at Emmaus which hangs in the chapel.[5] The undergraduate art committee had held a competition among several invited artists, and Richards was chosen as winner.

Well before becoming a college, the hall had the satisfaction of getting itself included among the societies entitled in turn to elect a proctor. Dr Moore had been senior proctor for 1871/2, the nominee of the five halls which still survived, but since 1889

---

[3] Secretary for administration of the university 1966–72; subsequently bursar and fellow of Corpus Christi College.

[4] For a full description, with photographs, see *SEHM* (1957–8), 40–7.

[5] For a note recalling the circumstances and citing some appreciations see *SEHM* (1958–9), 41–3. The original sketches submitted by the artist are kept in the antechapel.

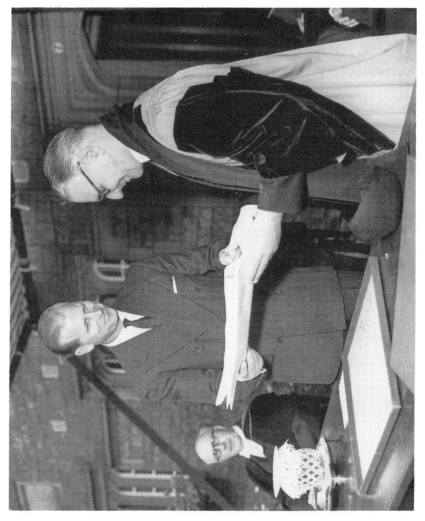

14. The Duke of Edinburgh presents the charter to Principal Kelly while Dr Emden looks on

the hall had voted with Queen's at proctorial elections, being effectively disfranchised by the vastly superior voting-strength of the college. In 1954, however, in response to lobbying by the principal and the heads of similarly deprived societies, the proctorial cycle was revised, and a new constituency consisting of (*a*) the hall and (*b*) St Peter's and St Antony's was created; later it was paired with St Peter's alone. In the period covered by this chapter its turn to elect came round twice, D. C. M. Yardley (fellow in jurisprudence) serving as senior proctor in 1965/6, and J. C. B. Gosling (fellow in philosophy: later principal) as senior proctor in 1977/8.

III

While these constitutional reforms were being prepared, the hall was moving steadily to a less centralized, more democratic style of administration. A straw in the wind was the omission, in early October 1951, of the promise to obey the principal[6] from the declaration made by the first new fellow to be admitted. About the same time the vice-principalship was made a largely honorific office (except during the absence or incapacity of the principal), with the disciplinary and other functions traditionally vested in it being shared out among a dean, a junior dean, and a dean of degrees. The first new-style vice-principal was the senior fellow, H. M. N. H. Irving; when he left Oxford in 1961, the office was made a rotating one, normally held for three years by a senior fellow who had not already held it. The first dean and junior dean were the Revd J. McManners (he was also chaplain) and E. G. (later the Revd) Midgley. On McManners's departure to Australia in 1956 Midgley succeeded him, and remained dean for some twenty-two years. Living in college and closely identified with its life, he thus brought to his task a rarely matched continuity and expertise. Another office which loomed even larger in the fifties and early sixties than subsequently was the senior tutorship; its holder was a senior fellow, C. W. F. R. Gullick. As the principal concerned himself for several years (though decreasingly) with admissions and relied heavily on Gullick's advice, he was in effect admissions tutor too. As such he left a distinctive impress on the intake of freshmen, for

---

[6] See above p. 114.

he had an unashamed bias in favour of sportsmen and all-rounders as commoners.

Even more striking was the emergence and expanding role of the bursarship. The half-time bursar appointed by Emden in 1949[7] had not been a fellow and had worked largely under his direction, but when he retired in 1953 the hall decided that it needed a bursar with fuller initiative who should be a full member of the governing body, responsible for both its domestic economy and its investments. Its choice fell on R. E. Alton, himself an aularian, who was lecturer in English at the time and was already acquiring skill as a palaeographer. Elected almost immediately to a fellowship, he continued as domestic bursar until 1970, as finance bursar until 1979. Exceptionally experienced as he thus became, he played a leading part in the various developments undertaken by the college in this period, and was particularly successful in representing it in critical financial negotiations with the university.

While the impulse behind these changes was to spread responsibility as widely as was practicable, it is ironical that the impression formed by an incoming fellow in the early sixties was that the college was run by a cabal of three powerful officers—the senior tutor, the dean, and the bursar—with the principal liaising with each in the not too distant background. But decentralization had not come to a halt. In the mid-sixties the governing body, which had functioned somewhat amateurishly in the years immediately following the granting of the charter (none of its members had direct experience of how colleges operated), reorganized its procedures and set up a system of standing committees to supervise the several aspects of the college's internal life and business. Well before this the selection of commoners had passed from the principal to committees of faculty tutors, and in 1966 an admissions tutor (E. R. Oxburgh), with an embryonic admissions office, was appointed with the task of co-ordinating the whole admissions process. Although rid of admissions, the senior tutorship (held in sucession by J. C. B. Gosling, J. Hackney, A. B. Worden, and K. H. Segar) was becoming an ever-busier office, not least because of the growing importance of the inter-college senior tutors' committee. A further step in devolution was taken in 1970 when, coincident with the opening of the new buildings, a full-time

---

[7] See above p. 128.

domestic bursar (Rear-Admiral G. C. Leslie) was appointed with responsibility, under a strong bursarial committee, for the entire domestic management of the college, including the steadily growing business of vacation conferences.

IV

Throughout the whole of Kelly's principalship the hall was making determined efforts to break out of its constricted site and acquire ampler buildings of every kind. A start was made in October 1952 when the residential portions of Nos. 49–52 High Street, leased from Magdalen in 1950[8] and now joined up to form a large annexe, were brought into occupation as the Besse Building (so named because its adaptation and furnishing were paid for out of Antonin Besse's benefaction).[9] Access to it was by a stately portal[10] (since removed) at the head of a flight of steps leading up from the area north of Staircase 8; when they first stepped through it, the principal and fellows had a thrill akin (one would surmise) to that of Columbus taking possession of the New World. When opened, the building provided bed-sitters for thirty-three students, flats for a married fellow and a married scout, and, on the first floor overlooking High Street, a spacious social room which the old members had furnished in commemoration of A. B. Emden's principalship.[11] This Emden Room was, for reasons of practical convenience, transferred in 1958 to its present position in the old quadrangle, the student library it there displaced being switched to the room in the Besse Building.

Next, the college took steps both to consolidate its hold on the High Street properties it held on lease and to prepare the way for the much more ambitious expansion it was now planning. First in 1955 it purchased from New College, for £10,000, the freehold of Nos. 55, 55a, and 56 High Street, opposite the Eastgate Hotel. After they had been structurally linked with the Besse Building, these houses were brought into occupation in 1957 and 1958, and provided rooms for some twenty-seven additional students. Then in 1959 it purchased from Magdalen, for £18,500, the freehold of the Masonic buildings, and shortly after cleared the way for the

[8] See above p. 126.   [9] See above p. 127.
[10] For photographs see *SEHM* (1952), facing p. 66.
[11] For the original Emden Room see *SEHM* (1953), 9–10 (with photograph).

development of the site by persuading the masonic lodges to surrender their subleases on the property, due to run until 2005, for £10,000. These delicate negotiations were smoothed by information released by two fellows who belonged to the brotherhood. Finally, in 1962 it bought from Magdalen for £124,246 (a price which took account of several shops at street level) the freehold of the whole line of houses forming Nos. 46–52 High Street. When these bold acquisitions were completed, it stood possessed of a site several times larger than the original quadrangle.

The grand design to which these purchases were the necessary prelude was, in addition to the remodelling of Nos. 46–8 High Street, the erection on the Masonic site of an elaborate complex of new buildings, social and residential. The decision to build afresh, demolishing rather than modifying and adapting the existing structures, was probably the most momentous one the hall had ever taken. There were some who judged it foolhardy and irresponsible, but the majority were fired by faith in the future. But progress had to be slow. Although the Forum restaurant's lease of the site expired in September 1962, the whole project was held up for several years, first because of delays in getting the architectural plans approved by the city, and then because the college felt obliged to part company with its original architect. Meanwhile its confidence was boosted in July 1961 when the Wolfson Foundation, with the director of which the principal had deliberately established close contacts in 1958 when the Wolfson chair of metallurgy was allocated to it, announced that it proposed to make it a grant of £120,000, specifically earmarked for a dining-hall, kitchens, and common rooms. In reaching its decision the Foundation was responding to a personal intervention of the visitor (Harold Macmillan, then prime minister) prompted by the principal, who had been warned that its interest was veering in another direction. For its part the governing body in 1962 launched a New Buildings appeal, with a target of £350,000; it reactivated this in 1965 with the aid of a firm of professional fund-raisers.

Operations were at last started in mid-summer 1965, when the Masonic buildings and parts of the High Street houses were demolished. From this point work went steadily, if noisily, ahead, with a giant yellow crane, visible from Magdalen bridge to Carfax, dominating the area; the chaos of pile-drivers, excavating machines, and concrete-pourers distracted dons and students alike

15. Nos. 46–56 High Street, with the Besse Building (marked by three armorial shields) in the right half

for months from their legitimate pursuits. The plans had been prepared by the college's new architect, Gilbert Howes, of the firm of Kenneth Stevens and Partners. The Kelly and Emden blocks were ready for occupation by Michaelmas term 1969, the college dinner was held for the first time in the Wolfson hall on 15 January 1970,[12] and the main buildings were formally declared open by Lady Edith Wolfson, in the presence of the visitor and Sir Isaac Wolfson, at a luncheon held in the hall on Friday 26 June 1970. The building-programme was brought to a close by the completion of White Hall (so named after the academical hall which had occupied the site in the middle ages)[13] in 1974, of the redesigned houses Nos. 46 and 47 High Street in 1975, and of the refurbished nineteenth-century town house known as Staircase 8 in 1976. Towards the cost of these constructions the appeals of 1961 and 1965 had contributed some £135,000, while a 'Completion Appeal' started in 1972 had produced a further £125,000.

For most of this period the college made use of two houses in north Oxford, one in Linton Road of which it held the remainder of a lease, and the other at Capel Close which it had received as a bequest from an old member. In addition it took a twenty-one-year lease in 1965 from Magdalen of No. 7 Long Wall, adapting it as a graduate centre housing six graduates and a middle common room. Even so its appetite for residential accommodation remained unsatisfied. Learning that the Society of St John the Evangelist (the Cowley Fathers) planned to relinquish its famous monastic house in Marston Street, the principal and the bursar persuaded the college to put in a bid for it early in 1979. When the Society decided to sell the property to the Anglican theological college, St Stephen's House, the governing body switched its bid to the substantial premises in Norham Gardens shortly to be vacated by the theological college. The negotiations were successfully concluded a few months after Kelly's retirement at the end of July; the newly acquired annexe, renamed Norham St Edmund, as well as possessing a substantial garden, provided rooms on both sides of the road for some fifty undergraduates, twelve graduates, and several married students in separate maisonettes; it also had a handsome common room, and flats for a resident don and a caretaker. The pretty chapel, in which the present writer had

[12] For a photograph see *SEHM* (1969–70), facing p. 7.
[13] See above pp. 15–17; 22–5.

worshipped four times daily in the early thirties, was converted into a multi-gym, where students might build themselves up physically rather than spiritually. The cost of £700,000 was met out of A. B. Emden's legacy, an anonymous benefaction of £200,000, and £300,000 raised by a special appeal to old members.

V

Parallel with these building developments, the discussions about possible closer association of St Peter-in-the-East with the college, which had dragged on fitfully for at least two decades, were in 1966 brought to a successful conclusion. Under an order in council uniting the three benefices of St Mary the Virgin, St Cross, and St Peter's, the college was assigned the use of the church and its churchyard (the freehold of which remained vested with the church authorities) 'for its religious and educational purposes'. The initial proposal of the bishop of Oxford (H. J. Carpenter) that the church should become the college chapel was turned down as impracticable, but the counter-suggestion (first put forward by the Revd H. E. J. Cowdrey, chaplain and fellow-librarian) that it should be transformed into a library met with the approval of both parties.

The process of conversion[14] proved a lengthy one, and was supervised by a committee chaired by J. Hackney (law fellow and—at the time—librarian). To start with, there were complicated discussions, not lacking moments of comedy, between a college which had never before saddled itself with a redundant church, and a diocesan authority which had not previously handed over one for such a conversion. There was also much toing and froing as the college tried, with considerable success as it transpired, to dispose at once discreetly and devoutly of the bells, the pulpit, the font, the organ, the pews. The fabric itself, including the tower, needed thorough restoration (architect J. R. Allen), and as a preliminary to this an extensive excavation of the floor was carried out by archaeologists (led by D. S. Sturdy, of Liverpool university); this established the exact outline of the Norman building, with some hints of its Saxon predecessor. A noteworthy feature was the renovated tower, on which the eroded bosses beneath the parapet were replaced by heads (sculpted by Michael

---

[14] For summary reports see *SEHM* (1965–6), 7–8; (1966–7), 10; (1967–8), 6–7; (1968–9), 11–12.

Groser) gently caricaturing several officers of the college, the architect and the sculptor, and masons and others connected with the building firm.[15] The churchyard was redesigned as a garden, with newly drawn paths leading to the old quadrangle; a cohort of undergraduate volunteers had helped to dig up and remove most of the gravestones, while a scholarly old member (Revd J. S. Reynolds) had compiled a record of the inscriptions both inside the church and in the churchyard.

The library was opened for use in Michaelmas term 1970, and was completed (with the roof painted in glowing red and yellow—a gift from A. B. Emden) by Christmas. The crypt had also been restored, and the practice was started of celebrating the eucharist there on appropriate days. Although the college had spent approximately £80,000 (towards which it received a contribution of £7,500 from the Historic Churches Fund), it at last possessed a library adequate to its needs, as well as ranking among the more beautiful in Oxford. To provide for its supervision the governing body had already, in 1966, for the first time appointed a full-time, professionally trained assistant librarian.

VI

Two policies which were vigorously pursued, the first in the fifties and early sixties and the second throughout the whole of this period, were the improvement of the fellows' conditions and the enlargement and diversification of the fellowship. A regular high table, the lack of which the fellows had been painfully conscious of before 1951, was started almost immediately. It was thought prudent to sound the undergraduates; to the dons' relief, their reaction was unmixed delight at no longer having to dine in close contiguity with them. The high table was in full use by 2 June 1953, when a coronation banquet was held in the dining-hall and the new queen was toasted by the fellows (those entitled to do so wearing decorations or medals) and such of the undergraduates as had not made their way to the celebrations in London. As well as being the senior common room, the Old Library became, and for twenty years remained, the meeting-place of the governing body. Two further commodious rooms, with ancillary offices, were set apart

---

[15] For the identities of all the 'faces facing down' see *SEHM* (1969–70), 9–10.

for the fellows in the new buildings. Starting early in 1953, and intensified when the new bursar took over the financial reins later that year, strenuous and eventually successful efforts were made to devise co-ordinated salary scales for the fellows and to keep them in line with those of other colleges. The fees paid for outside tuition were similarly raised to the generally accepted levels.

The hall had five fellows in 1951 when Kelly took over as principal, and in his first term he admitted a sixth to office. The six had become eleven by February 1957, when the charter declared 'the members of the first governing body', along with the principal, to be H. M. N. H. Irving (inorganic chemistry), G. D. Ramsay (modern history), R. Fargher (French), C. F. W. R. Gullick (geography), Revd E. G. Midgley (English literature), D. C. M. Yardley (jurisprudence), R. E. Alton (bursar), G. W. Series (physics), R. B. Mitchell (English language), G. R. Allen (economics), and Revd H. E. J. Cowdrey (modern history: also chaplain). The number continued to rise steadily, and had reached thirty-eight (several of international repute) by mid-summer 1979. The increase was much greater relatively than the increase of student numbers during the period; it was in part aimed at cutting down the hall's often criticized over-dependence on the tutorial resources of other societies, in part also at enabling it to make its own appropriate, independent contribution to the university. The enhanced total included, as well as the domestic bursar, several professorial and junior research fellows. The first professorial fellow (W. Hume-Rothery, FRS) was elected in 1958, when the newly founded Wolfson chair of metallurgy was allocated to the college, and the first junior research fellow (A. W. B. Simpson)[16] in 1954. The latter's fellowship was funded out of a benefaction given over five successive years by an anonymous admirer of the hall who claimed to have enjoyed close friendship with all its principals since Moore; on his death in 1959 he was revealed to be canon Claude Jenkins,[17] professor of church history, a figure of legendary learning and eccentricity.

Even more striking was the range of disciplines covered by this greatly expanded fellowship. Although it effectively dropped theology, the college's interest in what had been its traditional fields

---

[16] Since 1987 professor of law at the university of Michigan.
[17] For a vivid and accurate portrayal of him see *The Times* (19 Jan. 1959); also *Obituaries from The Times 1951–60* (Reading, 1979), 389–90.

remained undiminished. Indeed, it created additional fellowships in English literature, modern languages, and geography, and inaugurated fellowships in subjects for which it had hitherto relied on lecturerships—jurisprudence, economics, politics, English language, and mathematics. On the other hand, it now became increasingly concerned for the natural sciences, a field previously represented by a single fellowship and a handful of lecturerships. Fellowships were started in physics in 1955, and in 1959 in engineering (this was the first teaching fellowship in the subject offered by any college). By 1978/9 this shift in emphasis had become unmistakable, with two tutorial fellowships in physics, two in chemistry, two in engineering, one in metallurgy, one in psychology, one in physiology, and two in geology; in addition, there were two professorial fellowships in metallurgy, and one in clinical neurology. As if to balance it, the college, with the help of funds provided by the Oxford automotive industry, set up a senior research fellowship in industrial relations, with A. I. Marsh as its holder, in 1964, and in 1978 strengthened the ties it had been forming at the student level with the Ruskin School of Drawing by electing the Ruskin master (P. B. Morsberger) to a professorial fellowship.

In 1966 St Edmund Hall and Fitzwilliam College, Cambridge, a much more youthful society but one which also had recently obtained a charter, entered upon what quickly proved to be a mutually beneficial and amicable alliance as sister colleges.

VII

At the beginning of this period the hall counted as one of the poorest societies in Oxford, with capital investments of no more than £95,000 and an endowment income well below the level at which colleges were required by the university to contribute to central funds. Before long it lost even the trickle of subsidies that flowed to it from outside. Thus in 1959, in exchange for a lump sum of £1,000, it voluntarily commuted, as an embarrassing survival of an earlier age, the annual charge on the long-suffering rectory of Gatcombe to which it was legally entitled,[18] while the

---

[18] See above p. 102. For its extinction see *SEHM* (1958-9), 7-8.

grant of £150 a year provided by Queen's for exhibitions lapsed in 1962.

Despite this handicap it almost immediately (the starting-point was the arrival of the new bursar in 1953) embarked upon, and consistently maintained, boldly expansionist financial policies. Had it followed more timorous courses, it could never have undertaken the great enlargement of site, buildings, and teaching resources which it was determined to carry through. It received several valuable benefactions in addition to those already mentioned: for example, the Hoover Foundation gave £35,000 earmarked for new buildings, and the Colocotronis family (three members of which had been undergraduates) provided the first floor of White Hall. As has been noted, it raised considerable sums by public appeals, and in 1958 it formed fruitful ties with the Armourers and Brasiers' Company in the city of London, which funded annual awards in metallurgy and related subjects. Another who endowed awards in the science of metals, and was to become a splendid benefactor, was the Swiss engineer and philanthropist, Frederick Brockhues, who had got to know and become a close friend of A. B. Emden in the latter's old age. In large measure, however, the college had to finance its ambitious, but inevitable, development programme from its own resources. Similarly, while two or three of the growing number of fellowships could be subsidized in part by, for example, the Besse and the Claude Jenkins benefactions, the funding of the college (as distinct from the university) element in the majority had to come from current revenue.

It was therefore in the college's interest to maximize its income by keeping its student numbers as high as was consistent with academic standards and the preservation of the intimate collegiate atmosphere it valued, and also to accept each year reasonable quotas of entrants in the subjects represented by tutorial fellowships. It could not afford the luxury of academic posts (other than research fellowships) which did not contribute in some measure to their cost. From the late fifties onwards, particularly after it had acquired up-to-date buildings and adequate dining facilities, it benefited increasingly from the inflow of fresh money from conferences held in the vacations. By prudently investing any surpluses it substantially augmented the capital at its disposal; as its programme of expansion got under way, it was prepared to sink a large proportion of this in freehold sites and buildings. Along with six other poorly endowed colleges it received from the university's college contributions fund very substantial grants (amounting in its case to £500,000) between 1969 and 1978. The stated objective of these grants, which were made at the prompting of the report of the Franks commission of inquiry (1966), was to enlarge the permanent endowment of each of the recipient colleges to £600,000, but the decree authorizing them specifically allowed them to be used for building provided any amount so used was replaced over a period of fifty years. In view of what it considered its paramount needs the college had no hesitation in availing itself of this discretion. As a result, although its general financial position was very much healthier in 1978/9 than in 1951/2 and it at last possessed an extensive freehold site and buildings, it still lagged behind the great majority of colleges in actual capital endowment.

VIII

For reasons already noted the college was steadily growing in student numbers from 1951 to 1978. There were some 230 undergraduates and graduates in residence in 1951/2, 382 in 1964/5, 420 in 1974/5, and 427 in 1978/9. In this last year it was the seventh largest among those colleges traditionally admitting men, being surpassed in size by St Catherine's (540), New College (449), Christ Church (453), Wadham (448), Merton (444), and Balliol (435).

A feature of this growth was the marked increase in the number and range of graduate students. In the immediate post-war years these had amounted to a handful, most of them aiming at qualifications for teaching. Now, however, the college was keeping on more of its abler graduates, and was accepting a growing number of graduates of other universities, including a sprinkling from overseas, in order to work for higher degrees. The provision of a more spacious graduate common room than the one started at 7 Long Wall in 1965 became urgently necessary. Thus when the new JCR was opened beneath and west of the Emden building in 1970, the earlier JCR on the ground floor of the north range of the old quadrangle was set apart as a middle common room with its own bar and facilities. The first president of the MCR (A. W. Bower) was elected in 1965, when R. B. Mitchell represented the senior common room as its senior member. Before long, however, the office of tutor for graduates was created to liaise with the growing army of graduate students. In the late sixties and seventies it was held in succession by K. H. Segar, N. J. Stone, and R. B. Mitchell.

Throughout these decades the college's academic fortunes, as statistically illustrated by the so-called Norrington tables comparing the performance of all the colleges in finals, fluctuated erratically. If in 1977 it was bumping along at the bottom of the table, in 1978 it soared to fourth place, with twenty-three firsts to its credit, as well as several university awards and prizes. The general thrust, however, was upwards, results overall being better in the sixties than in the fifties, and in the seventies than in the sixties. A by-product of this was the sharply rising number of its graduates appointed to academic posts at Oxford and other universities, at home and overseas. The college was also an enterprising centre of music, drama, and the arts; its JCR art committee was exceptionally active, building up (with advice from its senior member, R. E. Alton) a valuable and frequently exhibited collection of pictures. Even more remarkable was the number of its students who were later to achieve distinction in the world of the arts. They included Gordon Crosse and Nigel Osborne, the composers; Jesse Allen, the California-based painter; the poet Kevin Crossley-Holland; John Cox, producer of opera and plays; Patrick Garland, director of plays and films; and Terry Jones, versatile artist in both films and television.

In sport the hall's performance had been on the upgrade before and immediately after the war. Now it was enjoying an era of unprecedented success. This was in spite of the fact that it had no playing-fields (a lack which, admittedly, had compensating advantages), but rented grounds in the University Parks, and only acquired a boat-house of its own in 1969. Its first eight was rarely out of the first division of Eights; year after year it sent boats to Henley and other regattas. The intercollegiate sporting cups, notably for rugby, football, and athletics, were repeatedly captured by its teams. No college during these years produced so many outstanding sportsmen: J. L. Fage (rowing), E. J. H. Gould (rugby and rowing), R. G. Lunn (football), P. G. Robbins (rugby), and M. J. K. Smith (rugby and cricket) were only a few of the scores of hall men who achieved university, sometimes nation-wide, recognition. The *annus mirabilis* was 1959, when the college not only went head of the river for the first time, but carried away the rugby, football, and athletic cups. The result was a crop of embarrassingly complimentary articles in the London press, the *Sunday Times* eloquently extolling 'a sporting achievement unequalled in university history'. This stung the *Oxford Magazine* into printing a mean-spirited paragraph questioning the college's admissions policy. The following week the principal hit back with a light-hearted riposte intended to show that the *Magazine* had got its facts wrong.[19] The incident was over almost as soon as it had begun; but it gave the fellows, most of whom valued sporting successes as good for corporate morale, a sharp reminder that academic standards must be seen to be paramount.

In spite of its swollen population the strong community spirit which had marked the hall from at any rate the late nineteenth century continued undiminished, and was perhaps even enhanced. Just as the constricted old quadrangle had tended to foster it, so the happy chance that the sprawling new buildings were grouped around interrelated small open areas helped to keep it going. The establishment of a thriving buttery bar at the bottom of Staircases 1 and 2 also helped. In most years this spirit found a celebratory outlet in a summer ball at the end of Trinity term, held at first in a marquee in the quadrangle but later in the Wolfson dining-hall. Organized by efficient student committees, these balls were almost all markedly successful, despite the fact that the prices of tickets invariably seemed, to senior members at any rate, far beyond the undergraduate pocket. By contrast the chapel, which throughout the nineteenth and first half of the twentieth century had been a focal-point of hall life, was now settling down to a steadily diminishing role—as much the reflection of the spirit of contemporary Oxford as of the altered character of the college's membership. Not only were numbers attending in steep decline, but in the late sixties the pattern of twice-daily services, traditional since the opening of the chapel, was abandoned. A more positive break with tradition was the start, in May 1967, of periodical celebrations in the chapel of mass according to the Roman Catholic rite. A notable occasion was Sunday 20 October 1972 when the celebrant was cardinal Leo Jozef Suenens, primate of Belgium, who

---

[19] See *OM* 77 (4 June 1959), 454 for the attack, and 77 (18 June 1959), 474, for the reply.

as university preacher was staying in the principal's lodgings and expressed the wish to say mass in the chapel after his sermon.

The post-war epoch was a time when relations between senior and junior members in the colleges generally were becoming even closer than they had earlier been; this went far to explain the relatively mild impact on Oxford of the student troubles of the late sixties and early seventies. The hall's dons were not behindhand in promoting an atmosphere of camaraderie. The demand was being pressed, however, by student activists for more formalized arrangements, the prize aimed at being membership of governing bodies and participation in 'decision-making'. To go some way to meet this the college set up a mixed committee of senior and junior members in 1968. Known as the college committee, it met at least twice a term to consider any matter affecting the life of the college; the JCR and MCR presidents were *ex-officio* members and had the right to attend, without a vote, meetings of the governing body at which the minutes of the committee were on the agenda. Later the right of junior members to *ad hoc* attendance at meetings of certain committees of the governing body, and on appropriate occasions of the governing body itself (again without a vote), was granted. In May 1974 a special statute was formally approved providing junior members with the legal right to a fair hearing when serious disciplinary action against them was being considered.

IX

In 1973 the governing body completely revised the original collegiate statutes of 1956. The new statutes, approved by the counsellors of state in council in February 1974, were more detailed and precise, and were intended to take account of altered practice in the colleges generally. An illustration was the provision of 'security of tenure' for fellows, i.e. their right, if re-elected after a probationary period of three years, to retain their fellowships until the retiring age. Under the 1956 statutes their appointment had been for seven years at a time, renewable at the discretion of the governing body. The new principle, later to be questioned by central government, was based on models of university statutes supplied by the university grants committee in the 1960s which were known in advance to have the approval of the privy council at the time. Another provision deserving note, this time as breaking with centuries-old tradition, stipulated that the college should have a chaplain, but studiously omitted the customary requirement that he should be a priest of the church of England and conduct services according to its prayer book. Apart from these, the statutes introduced no radical innovation. For this the college had to wait until 1976, when a small but revolutionary amendment was made to them.

As early as 1966 New College had declared its wish to open its doors to women. This started a lively debate as a result of which the university in 1972, with the consent of the women's colleges and as a limited experiment, permitted five hitherto male colleges (Brasenose, Hertford, Jesus, St Catherine's, and Wadham) to alter their statutes and accept about 100 women between them. By 1976 this pilot scheme was judged so successful that the university decided to abandon the attempt to control co-residence (as it was coming to be called) by withholding consent to changes in statutes designed to effect it. In the months following the great majority of the remaining men's colleges including St Edmund Hall, took steps to avail themselves of the freedom thus extended to them.

Since the early seventies the college had had women lecturers; this was legally possible because, while its statutes (like those of other men's colleges) led off with the restrictive clause 'No woman shall be a member of the college', a lecturer did not strictly count as a member. Even earlier, in 1970, the middle common room had begun offering associate membership to women members of the department of education who had been unable to find places in women's colleges owing to their quota being full. In June 1976 the momentous proposal was brought before the governing body that the clause excluding women should be deleted from the statutes, and consequential changes introduced elsewhere indicating that membership was open to them at every level equally with men. A two-thirds majority was required for the amendment of statutes, and with opinion sharply divided it was obtained by a narrow margin. At this point a temporary delay occurred because both the charter and certain deeds settling the relationship between the college and Queen's specifically defined it as a place of education for men members of the university.[20] While there was no difficulty in obtaining the necessary agreements, the drawing-up of a fresh

---

[20] See above pp. 131 (charter), 119 (Queen's).

deed and, more importantly, the special procedures prescribed for the amendment of the charter took up several months. These complicated preliminaries were, however, completed by Trinity term 1977, and the amendments to both charter and statutes were approved by the queen in council on 9 February 1978.

Immediately Vivien Mary Jones, elected in 1977 *faute de mieux* ? to a junior research lecturership, became St Edmund Hall's first woman junior research fellow. The new intake admitted in October 1978 included one woman graduate student (Elizabeth Butler), and many girls were candidates at the entrance-scholarship examinations in November–December. Some thirty-seven of these, among them two open scholars, joined the college in Michaelmas term 1979. Very early next year it elected a woman tutorial fellow (Ann Gaynor Taylor: physiology), with Vivien Jones the first of her sex (soon to be followed by others) to take her place at the high table and on the governing body, the first fellow too to be appointed tutor for women. Before long young women research students would sometimes hold office as junior deans and administer discipline to disorderly students.

The unpretentious academical hall which Oseney abbey started as an investment around 1300, a few yards from the church which Edmund of Abingdon had enriched with its lady chapel, had over the centuries been transformed beyond recognition. None of the astonishing changes it had undergone would have startled John of Cornwall, and all his successors to date but one, more than this implementation of the decision to go co-residential. Although he had helped to prepare the new order, it did not fall to the present writer either to admit the first women undergraduates or to take part in the election of the first woman tutorial fellow. Having reached the age of 70 on 13 April 1979, he retired as required by statute on the 31 July following. More than a year earlier, in March 1978, availing itself of the powers of pre-election provided by the 1974 statutes, the governing body, with the vice-principal (Revd E. G. Midgley) in the chair, had elected Sir Ieuan Maddock, CB, OBE, FRS, as his successor. A scientist with a distinguished career in the government service, he was the first principal to be chosen by the college itself, and the first to preside over it as a mixed community. He was also the first principal in almost seven hundred years to be formally admitted to office, not by the vice-chancellor, but by the vice-principal, at the first meeting of its governing body in October 1979.

Index

Names of principals are in small capitals

accounts 89, 91, 102, 104
admissions tutor 134, 135
AGLIONBY, JOHN 32, 34, 35
AIRAY, ADAM 38–40, 41, 43
Airay, Christopher 40, 43
ALLEN, GERALD BURTON 106–10, 111, 130
Allen, Jesse 146
altar-piece by Ceri Richards 132
Alton, R. E. 135, 139, 142, 144, 146
appeals 61, 104, 112, 120, 137, 139, 140
architects: J. R. Allen 140; R. Fielding Dodd 115; G. Howes 139; Bartholomew Peisley 47; Kenneth Stevens and Partners 139; H. G. Rogers 108; G. E. Street 85
Armourers and Brasiers' Company 144
art committee, JCR 132, 146
association of old members 109, 118

Balliol College 1, 43, 145
balls, summer 126, 147
BARROW, JOHN 80–3, 85
Bate, George 37, 41
baths 104, 108, 115
Berkeley, Sir William 37
Bermingham, Sir Brian de 4, 5; John de 4, 5, 14, 22; Roger de 4, 5
BERUGHDON, ROBERT 16, 18
Besse, Antonin 127, 136
Besse benefaction 127, 136, 144; Building 136
Bishop, Nicholas 15–17, 19–20, 25
Blackmore, Sir Richard 53
boat club 95–6

Book of Benefactors 61
Boswell, James 65
BOWSFIELD, THOMAS 33–4, 35, 38
BOYS, WILLIAM 5, 11
BRAITHWAITE, MILES 26, 27
Bramley vicarage 59, 61, 62, 67, 68
BRANTHWAITE, JOHN 80, 83, 85, 87
Brasenose College 9, 31, 149
Brewis, G. R. 103, 104
Brockhues, Frederick 144
BROKE, RICHARD 25, 39
Browne, J. T. 81, 82
BRYTON, WILLIAM 21
Burne-Jones, Sir Edward 85
bursar (domestic) 105, 110, 111, 112, 128, 135, 136, 142; (finance) 135, 139
bursary 107, 108, 112, 125
buttery 25, 55, 61, 147

Campbell, B. G. 132
Canterbury Building 115–17, 124
Capel Close, house at 139
Carleton, bishop George 32–3
Cave, Viscount 108
CAWSE, THOMAS 26
chapel 46, 47, 49, 53, 59, 62, 64, 85, 93, 105, 117, 123, 128, 147–8
Charles II 37, 41, 48
charter of incorporation 131, 135, 149, 150
Chase, Dr D. P. 90, 91
Chaucer, Geoffrey 1, 4
Cherry, Francis 53, 55
Christ Church 2, 28, 29, 83, 85, 110, 145
CLERK, PETER, *see* PAYNE
college committee 148
Colocotronis family 144
commission, royal (1850) 67, 78–9, 80–1; of inquiry (1872)

commission, royal (*cont.*):
  90, 91; statutory (1877) 91–3,
  98, 99, 100, 101; royal (1919)
  106, 109
common room, junior 95, 104, 105,
  107, 113, 122, 132, 137, 145;
  middle 139, 145, 149; senior
  114, 128, 137, 141–2, 145
COOKE, NICHOLAS 32
Corpus Christi College 43
cottage, the 33, 34, 35, 104, 105,
  108, 117
Cowdrey, Revd H. E. J. 140, 142
Cox, John 146
Cromwell, Oliver 37, 43
CRONSHAW, GEORGE BERNARD 10,
  111, 112
Crosse, Gordon 146
Crossley-Holland, Kevin 146
CROSTHWAITE, DR THOMAS 48
Crouch, Isaac 69–70, 72, 73, 74
Curzon of Kedleston, Lord 101,
  104, 105
CUTHBERTSON, JOHN 26

Dante 87, 89, 99
DARLEY, JOHN 21
Day, Sir Robin 124
deans 134, 135, 150
debating society 76, 77, 95, 96, 122
Denysson, William 28, 29
dining hall (old) 4, 41, 43, 53, 59,
  64, 93, 107, 110, 111, 117, 141;
  (Wolfson) 137, 139, 147
DIXON, GEORGE 62–4, 65, 68, 69,
  70
Donkin, William F. 77
DOWSON, WILLIAM 67

Edmund of Abingdon, St 6–10, 98,
  117, 150
EMDEN, A. B. 105, 107, 110,
  111–29, 131, 136, 140, 141;
  legacy of 129, 140
Emden block 139; Room 136
essay society 95
Exeter College 13, 15, 127

Farrer, Revd A. M. 115, 117
fellows 118, 119, 120, 121–2, 125,
  128, 130, 131, 132, 134, 136,
  142–3, 147, 148, 150; first
  collegiate 142; first honorary
  120; first women 150; junior
  research 142, 144, 150;
  professorial 137, 142, 143
FELTON, HENRY 57, 58
financial position 91, 105, 107,
  112, 143–5
Fitzwilliam College 143
Fleming, Sir Daniel 51, 52
Fleming, George 51, 52, 53
FOTHERGILL, GEORGE 61–2
Freind, John 43, 44
Frogley, Arthur 47
Fullmer, Charles H. 96–8

Garland, Patrick 146
Gatcombe rectory 68, 87, 91, 92,
  102, 103, 104, 112, 143
Gladstone, W. E. 76, 80
Gloucester Hall 31
GOSLING, J. C. B. 134, 135
graduates, tutor for 146
GRAYSON, ANTHONY 67
Grayson, Cecil 124
Groser, Michael 140–1
Gullick, C. F. W. R. 125, 134

Hackney, J. 135, 140
Halifax, earl of 131
Halton, Dr Timothy 46, 48
HAMSTERLEY, WILLIAM 13
Hart Hall 43
Hearne, Thomas 33, 46, 48 n., 49,
  51, 52, 53, 55, 56, 57, 58, 59,
  117
Hearne Room 55, 117, 128
Henry VIII 11, 27, 28
Hertford College 64, 91, 103, 149
High Street houses 115, 126, 127,
  136–9
high table 114, 123, 141, 150
Higson, John 59, 63–4, 65
Hill, John 67, 69, 73, 74–6, 78, 79,
  83

Historic Churches Fund 141
Holme, Dr George 68
Hooknorton, abbot Thomas 23
Hoover Foundation 144
Hunt, H. J. 114
Huntingdon, countess of 63, 65
Hus, John 19

investments 91, 112, 118, 125, 135,
    143–5

Jenkins, canon Claude 142, 144
Jenkins, David 33–4
Jesus College 149
JOHN DE BERE 11, 13
JOHN OF CORNWALL 1, 11, 13, 14,
    150
JOHNSON, PHILIP 31, 32
Johnson, Dr Samuel 64, 65
Jones, Terry 146

Keble, John 81, 85
Keble College 94, 101, 127, 130
KELLY, JOHN N. D. 113, 120, 124,
    126, 127, 130–50
Kennett, White 49, 52, 53
Kettlewell, John 53
kitchen 2, 23, 25, 61, 107, 137

LANCASTER, THOMAS 30–1
Lang, archbishop Cosmo Gordon
    117
latrines 16, 22, 105, 117
Laud, William 38
lecturers 83, 89, 113–14, 125–6,
    149
LEE, THOMAS 24–5, 39
library (old) 47, 53, 55, 93, 105,
    117, 128, 141; (undergraduate)
    107, 108, 136; (in St Peter's)
    140–1
Liddon, Henry Parry 81–2, 83–6
Lincoln College 53, 111, 127
Linton Road (annexe) 139
Little St Edmund Hall 9
Littleton, Sir Thomas 53
Loggan, David 25, 69
Lollardy, Lollards 17–19

Long Wall, No. 7 139
LUC (LUKE), ROBERT 11, 13, 14

McManners, Revd John 125, 134
Macmillan, Harold 137
MADDOCK, Sir IEUAN 150
Magazine, St Edmund Hall 107
Magdalen College 25, 34, 35, 39,
    43, 105, 108, 115, 120, 126,
    136, 137, 139
Magdalen Hall 26, 31, 39, 46, 58,
    59, 78, 79
Magrath, J. R. 92–3, 99
Malan, Solomon Caesar 77
Masonic Buildings 120, 126,
    136–7
Merton College 1, 37, 92, 126, 127,
    145
Methuen, John 44
Midgley, Revd E. G. 134, 142, 150
MILL, JOHN 48–53, 55, 56, 57
Mitchell, R. B. 142, 145, 146
MOORE, EDWARD 87–102, 130,
    132, 142
Morris, William 85

New College 37, 44, 46, 47, 117,
    136, 145
New Inn Hall 39, 43, 91
New Leiger book 48, 49
Newman, cardinal J. H. 80, 82
Nicholas, Matthew 37
Nichols, Peter 124
Norham St Edmund 139–40

Oldham, John 53
Ollard, Revd S. L. 89, 95, 100, 103,
    120
Onslow, Sir Richard 53
organ 85, 117
Oriel College 43, 92
Oronhyatekha, Peter 83
Osborne, Nigel 146
Oseney abbey 1, 2, 3, 4, 5, 6, 11,
    13, 14, 15, 17, 21, 22, 23, 24, 25,
    26, 27, 28, 150

PATENSON, WILLIAM 26
PAYNE (or CLERK), PETER 16–20
PEARSON, THOMAS 55, 56–7
Pembroke College 43, 106, 127
pension arrangements 109, 114, 125
PENTON, STEPHEN 44, 46–8, 53, 117
PEYRSON, THOMAS 27, 28
Philip, duke of Edinburgh 132
porter's lodge 107
POTTER, BARNABAS 35
principal's lodgings 23, 38, 49, 59, 62, 69, 89, 107, 128
proctorship 24, 87, 132–4
PULLEN, NICHOLAS 32
Pusey, Dr E. B. 81, 85
PYTTES, JOHN 26

Queen's College 5, 13, 17, 21, 26–119 *passim*, 122, 130, 131, 132, 134, 149; composition of university with 29, 31, 38

RAWLINSON, JOHN 32, 35, 36, 37, 38
Reynolds, Revd J. S. 141
ROBERTSON, WILLIAM 27
ROBINSON, HENRY 32, 33
Royal Society 37, 59
RUDDE, RALPH 28, 29, 30
RUMWORTH, HENRY 12, 13, 15, 16
Ruskin School of Drawing 143

St Alban Hall 90, 91
St Antony's College 127, 134
St Catherine's College 124, 130, 145,149
St Edmund, Latin Hymn of 115
St Edmund's day 7, 98, 110, 120
St Frideswide's priory 2, 17, 28
St Hilda's Hall (College) 9, 105
St Hugh Hall 22, 23, 24, 25
St Hugh's College 125
St John's hospital 2, 4, 22, 23, 25
St Mary Hall 43, 46, 90, 91
St Peter-in-the-East 4, 6, 9, 10, 44, 55, 126–7, 140–1, 150

St Peter's Hall (College) 108, 121, 124, 127, 130, 134
Scholes, Percy A. 100
senior tutor 103, 128, 134, 135
SHAW, THOMAS 58–61
Sheldonian Theatre 47, 48, 87, 102
six students, affair of the 63–5
Spencer, Edward 65, 70, 74
sport 95–8, 109–10, 113, 122, 146–7; eminent exponents of 146
Stainer, Sir John 83
statutes, aularian 3, 36; Laudian 38; of 1913 101–2, 104, 109; of 1926 109; of 1937 114, 118–20, 128, 130; interim (1952) 131; of 1957 131–2; of 1973 148–9
Streeter, Provost B. H. 118
students: academic performance 94–5, 100, 109, 124, 146; expenses 36, 37, 43–4, 52, 79, 90, 92, 107, 112–13, 124–5, 130; numbers 23, 27, 30, 33, 34, 35, 39, 43, 46, 53, 57–8, 59, 61, 63, 65, 68, 83, 93–4, 100, 104, 105, 107, 112–13, 121, 123–4, 145–6; social background 47, 64, 76, 94, 107, 112, 113, 124
Sturdy, D. S. 140
Suenens, cardinal Leo Jozef 147–8
Sykes, Professor Norman 121

TAYLOR, WILLIAM 16, 17, 18, 19
THAMYS, JOHN 21–3, 39
Thomas of Malmesbury 4, 5, 6
THOMPSON, GEORGE 67, 69
THOMPSON, WILLIAM 67, 68, 78, 80, 81
Thompson, Provost W. 81, 82
THROP 13
TOPPYNGE, OTTWELL 27
Tournour, David 24
trustees of the hall 106, 109, 110, 118, 119, 120, 125, 126, 127, 128, 130, 131
TULLIE, THOMAS 41–4, 46, 51, 53
tutors 103, 106, 113, 114–15, 118, 124, 127, 135

'unattached students' 90, 91, 92, 96
University College 1, 43, 79
UPTON, EDWARD 13, 15

Veale, Sir Douglas 120, 127
vice-principals 31, 43, 44, 46, 49,
    52–3, 58, 59, 63, 66, 67, 69, 78,
    79, 80, 81, 83–5, 89, 95, 98,
    100, 103, 107, 113, 134, 150
visitation of 1613 35–6

Wadham College 79, 96, 106, 109,
    127, 145, 149
Walmsley, Mr Justice 31, 34
Wand, bishop J. W. C. 100, 120,
    123
Wanley, Humphrey 53, 55
well, the 14, 108
Wesley, John 62, 65
Westfield College, London 121
Wheatley, Henry 67, 74

White Hall (medieval) 15–17, 19,
    22, 24, 25, 115; (part of new
    buildings) 15, 139
Whitefield, George 63, 64
WILLIAMS, HERBERT HENRY 103–6,
    111, 120
Williamson, Sir Joseph 44, 47
Wilson, bishop Daniel 69, 72–4
Wolfson, Sir Isaac and Lady 139
Wolfson chair of metallurgy 137,
    142
Wolfson Foundation 137
women, admission of 149–50
Wood, Anthony 9, 13, 21, 24, 25,
    32, 33, 35 n., 38, 39, 41 n.
Worcester College 127
Wyclif, John 17–19
Wylie, Rt Hon. Lord 124
WYSTOWE, HUMPHREY 26

Yardley, D. C. M. 134, 142